I'm so fortunate to have gotten to know the [illegible] "behind the mask" after her hilarious video took the internet by storm and reminded us all to LAUGH with abandon! Candace has a lot to teach the world about living joyfully, laughing loudly, and cherishing the small things that make life worth living!

—**PATRICIA HEATON,** Emmy Award-winning actress and producer

On May 21, 2016, I posted this on my Facebook page: "Have y'all seen this video of a lady finding such joy in her newly purchased Chewbacca mask? . . I'm willing to bet she's a believer. That kind of joy comes from a much deeper place . . ." What's interesting about the spring of 2016 is that I was in a deep depression when I came across that viral video. Looking back on it now, I know that the joy I saw in Candace flooded Light into my pit of despair and beckoned my spirit to rise out of the dark. As you read Candace Payne's story, you will see why she is able to find joy in the simple things. I know firsthand the power of joy in the midst of pain. That is why I believe that God has spread Candace's contagious, Light-shining spirit for the world to see at such a time as this.

—**MANDISA,** Contemporary Christian recording artist

If you think Candace Payne is nothing more than a viral video, you are sorely mistaken. I recently spent time listening to her life's story and was stunned by the unspeakable pain she has endured and the breathtaking triumphs she has experienced. Candace Payne is more than a mask, and I'm confident that her new book will cement her as a go-to inspirational voice for years to come.

—**JONATHAN MERRITT**, contributing writer for *The Atlantic*; author of *Learning to Speak God from Scratch*

Candace truly does have the gift of spreading joy, and that is something that the world needs more of at this time. I'm happy she's using her platform to make people smile. This book will open people's eyes to see joy in their own life. It makes me proud to be her friend.

—**SADIE ROBERTSON**, bestselling author, speaker, and founder of Live Original The Tour

Thanks to a viral Facebook video, the world got to see a glimpse of the joy and spirit of Candace Payne. I've been fortunate to know and feel that joy and spirit in person both before and after the video took over the internet. There's more to Candace than one video. Candace has a gift. A gift for living her life with a smile on her face and a shine in her heart. *Laugh It Up!* will give readers an insight into that smile and shine and hopefully help even more people find joy in everything they do in life. And real and true joy is the most infectious and viral thing on the planet. Let's spread it together.

—**BARRETT BABER**, country music artist and songwriter

Don't be fooled: Candace Payne is more than a laughing Chewbacca mask, and this book is more than stories to make you giggle. These profoundly rich and vulnerable pages are an invitation to drink deeply from the well of joy. Even in the lean seasons, Candace reminds readers, Joy is beckoning us out to play. These are words for the weary, the hopeless, the dreamers, the fighters, and everyone in between. *Laugh It Up!* is an invitation to come back home and embrace our birthright—joy. You will laugh, cry, and remember the long-forgotten gift of playfulness as you journey through these pages and find yourself coming home to hope. This book is a rare, life-giving gift for the soul.

—**JENNY SIMMONS**, musician, author of *Made Well* and *The Road to Becoming*

Candace is more than just a joyful person; she is a JOY-FILLED person who has a passion to make the world a better place. *Laugh It Up!* will remind you to find joy in the small moments and guide you on your way to become someone who experiences "defiant joy" and hope each day.

—**HAL DONALDSON**, president, Convoy of Hope

Laugh it up!

EMBRACE FREEDOM AND **EXPERIENCE** DEFIANT JOY

CANDACE PAYNE

Viral Sensation, Chewbacca Mom

ZONDERVAN

Laugh It Up!

Requests for information should be addressed to:
Zondervan, *3900 Sparks Dr. SE, Grand Rapids, Michigan 49546*

ISBN 978-0-310-35236-5 (audio)

ISBN 978-0-310-35167-2 (ebook)

Library of Congress Cataloging-in-Publication Data

Names: Payne, Candace, author.
Title: Laugh it up! : embrace freedom and experience defiant joy / Candace Payne.
Description: Grand Rapids, Michigan : Zondervan, [2017]
Identifiers: LCCN 2017031992 | ISBN 9780310350569 (softcover)
Subjects: LCSH: Joy. | Shame.
Classification: LCC BF575.H27 P39 2017 | DDC 152.4/2—dc23 LC record available at https://lccn.loc.gov/2017031992

Author is represented by Jana Burson at The Christopher Ferebee Agency, www.christopherferebee.com.

Cover design: Curt Diepenhorst
Cover photography: Meshali Mitchell Photo
Interior design: Kait Lamphere

First printing September 2017 / Printed in the United States of America

To anyone who has ever experienced, lost, or forgotten
what living a life full of joy feels and looks like.

To the one who feels overlooked, undervalued,
or has a chronic case of the Mondays.

To the ones who live fearlessly, without
shame, and find every opportunity to throw
their heads back and laugh it up . . .

I dedicate this book to you.

May you find joy in your journey
wherever it leads.

CONTENTS

Joy
IS A
FIGHTER.

BEHIND THE MASK

I don't know about you, but it's not every day I get to hang out at the Facebook headquarters while a British man in a Wookiee costume rides a bicycle next to me as I try to remember what it feels like to balance each pedal. Yet, that's exactly where I found myself.

Facebook had invited me because five days earlier I had visited Kohl's. Stay with me here; this will make sense in a minute. Kohl's is a department store that is sort of like Disney World for stay-at-home moms. I needed to return something as well as do some rare shopping for myself. I had just celebrated my thirty-seventh birthday (forty was looming ever closer), and I wanted yoga pants, acutely aware that I needed to be more conscious of my health and become more active. Yoga pants are forever a mystery to me—they seem perfectly designed to expose all the places where one has *lacked* to provide ample activity—but I thought if I "dressed the part," then maybe I would be inspired to work out more often.

Like most women, it takes more than one store to find exactly what I like. So when I wound up empty-handed in my yoga pants search, I headed to the toy section to look for something for my kiddos instead. If you're a mother, you're probably familiar with this routine. You set out to get something for yourself but end up placing aside your own wants to prioritize your family. This day, I walked through a customer-rampaged hot mess of a clearance aisle that looked like a war zone. In other words, it felt similar to my living room. Bending over to remove some debris, I accidentally bumped into a toy (further proof I needed those stinkin' yoga pants) and heard a glorious growl.

I chuckled a tiny bit—after I jumped two feet—and lifted a box up from the bottom shelf. There he was in all his fur-faced glory. A plastic mask of Chewbacca from *Star Wars*. When you put it on and opened your mouth, it let out the trademark Wookie noise. Impulsively, I knew I was *so* getting this. First of all, it was on clearance, and this momma is a sucker for a sale. (Also, I have a core belief that if it has a clearance sticker, you don't need to pray about it. That's God's approval stamp.) And second, it was Chewbacca, for goodness' sake.

I'm a *Star Wars* fanatic, and this intergalactic animal has long been a favorite of mine. One scene in particular makes me fall more in love with Chewbacca every time I watch it. In a galaxy far, far away, Princess Leia has just finished putting Chewie's best friend (and seemingly sole interpreter), Han Solo, in his place. Her insult is lacking in, shall we say, creative scripting—she calls Han Solo a "Laser Brain"—and Chewbacca makes these adorable chuckles with an agreeing head nod. Han Solo shoots back a stink eye and says, "Laugh it up, Fuzzball!"

So Chewbacca has become a symbol for me of joy and levity and laughter. He is like an overgrown teddy bear with luscious locks and bangs that could make any Texas hair-loving momma jealous. Known for his guttural grunts, I love how lighthearted and innocent he seems under the giant, brute exterior. How could you not love him? And how could you not love a mask that, when you open your mouth, makes you sound like him? Forget the yoga pants.

After checking out, I put the plastic bag with the Chewbacca toy mask in my car and ran a couple of other errands. This was the day I set aside to spend some of my birthday gift cards as I made my usual grocery-and-post-office run. But I didn't forget about the mask. Tribal drums might as well have been calling to me from the bag in the backseat because when I got in the car after spending my gift card balance and presenting email birthday coupons for fragranced lotions, hand soaps, and plug-in wall air fresheners, all I could think about was taking out that mask and playing with it a bit before my kids could confiscate it. I finally gave in, ripped through the Kohl's shopping bag like Christmas wrapping paper, and answered the call.

Using my phone to broadcast live to all my Facebook friends, I donned the mask for the next five minutes. But something unexpected happened when I opened my mouth and the mask let out a Wookiee growl: I laughed it up. Not just a chuckle or a giggle, but a serious laugh. The kind that makes your jaw and sides hurt. And I couldn't stop no matter how hard I tried. Finally, out of breath yet overjoyed, I knew I had to get back to adult-ing and pick up my kids from school, so I ended the video and went about my day.

A few minutes later, a blip came across my phone. The video had been shared. At first, it was just my friends list sharing the replay of that Facebook Live moment. But soon (and I mean very soon), it was being shared by people whose names and profile pictures I didn't recognize. I'd set my phone aside only to see another blip. And then five more. The notifications snowballed until I couldn't keep up with them. Before I went to bed that night, I had reached a million views on that silly video in my crossover vehicle. Which meant that one million people had laughed it up with me as well. I rested my head on my pillow in awe and with satisfaction, knowing I had enjoyed a good laugh and made others laugh as well. All because of a clearance Wookiee.

Let's just say, I never had buyer's remorse or wished I'd gotten the yoga pants after that.

But while I was sleeping, the video went viral. Actually, not just viral but super viral. Record-breaking viral. The most views of a Facebook Live video until that time was about 10 million from a BuzzFeed video. By the time I woke on Friday morning, my video had been viewed over 24 million times. My phone was cluttered with voicemails from media outlets wanting to interview me, Facebook friend requests, and texts from family and friends. That afternoon, I sat hitting the refresh button on the video and watched it jump from 250–500 thousand views every four minutes. As I sit writing this today, it has been viewed over 166 million times and shared over 3.5 million times.

That video changed my life in ways I didn't anticipate. But it also changed my name, thanks to the press.

At first, news outlets reported the story with statements like, "Texas mom breaks record with Chewbacca mask video" and BBC's "Mum in Chewbacca mask shatters Facebook Live record." (I sipped imaginary tea with a raised pinky after reading that one.) But one day, I noticed a surprising word combination emerging in headlines:

- "Why 'Chewbacca Mom' is the viral video we didn't know we needed."
- "What 'Chewbacca Mom' teaches us about happiness."
- "Chewbacca Mom's moment of joy becomes viral sensation."

I was just a mother of two living outside Dallas who wanted to purchase some yoga pants. And I still am. But suddenly masses of people were calling me by a new name: Chewbacca Mom. The label felt strange at first, but I didn't exactly mind being associated with my favorite cuddly character from *Star Wars*.

But more interesting than the name was the headlines' shift in focus. Not only was the name *Chewbacca Mom* popping up, but words like *joy* and *happiness* were showing up too. These reporters and commentators suddenly saw me as the embodiment of joy and glee, of smiles and laughter. That's not so bad, considering that joy has long been one of my favorite subjects. But what the many reporters and millions of watchers could not have possibly known is that the person behind the mask has spent her lifetime intentionally fighting *for* moments of laughter.

Unlike what many might assume, joy hasn't come easy in my life. I've had to fight for it through tears, economic hardships, disappointments, regrets, and shame. Behind the mask, I was someone who often felt given up on, overlooked, undervalued, and insignificant. I was a person with family stability issues and a less-than-perfect marriage who often struggled to figure out how to stretch our budget from one paycheck to another.

When the infectious laughter died down, Candace Payne was another person just like you.

I'm guessing you have been cut and bruised by sharp words and blunt disappointments. You've felt the pain from rejection and abandonment. You've had more than your share of tearful afternoons and sleepless nights. When people look in your direction, you often feel like they see through you. At times, you've poured out the very best of yourself with little return on investment. You've felt half an inch small, questioning your worth and value in the midst of the tiny timeline you occupy in the giant scope of all time and humanity.

Like me, you've put on a mask at some point in life, denying your true desires, wants, and identity. What would it look like for you to learn to laugh while wearing your mask? What would it mean for you to feel free enough to take that mask off and embrace who you already are? Like me, I bet you want to discover joy—the kind of joy that laughs, loves, and is defiant in the face of difficulty. The kind of joy that embraces the imperfect people we are and helps us heal our wounds and silences our deepest regrets.

When life punches you in the gut, it can be difficult to muster a smile—much less a laugh. I get it. My journey to becoming Chewbacca Mom was more than an overnight success. It's a path that you, too, can travel if you want. It will lead you to taking off your mask, finding freedom, and experiencing defiant joy.

So, open your heart, turn the page, and laugh it up, Fuzzball.

Joy
LIKES TO
PLAY.

Chapter 1

FINDING THE HAPPY IN HOMELESS

I bounced up the stairs of the two-star Budget Suites, excited to sleep in a bed for the first time in weeks. My family had been in transition for most of my childhood. We moved multiple times, and I attended multiple elementary schools (at times, switching teachers and towns two to three times a school year). Each time, I followed with the flow of our family's nomadic rhythm. Upon making new friends (which never came easy to me, being forever the "new kid" in school), I would inevitably face a daunting question: "Why does your family move so much?" How I longed to have a definitive answer.

As a child, all I knew was that times were tough for my family. My parents had four children, two boys and two girls. By the time they had me, their fourth child who came as a bit of an unplanned shock, they were already raising a ten-, nine-, and seven-year-old. My parents were doing the best they could with what they had. Raising a family of six (plus a dog) demands finding creative ways to save money wherever possible. My family would embrace opportunities to eat out at nice restaurants only if they knew we could dine on a good special. Yet, as children, we never knew if we were going to eat canned beans and weenies or delicious Red Lobster cheddar biscuits and unlimited shrimp and lobster from week to week. We shifted from feast to famine on a semi-regular basis. Fried spam sandwiches and goulash were more the norm. Anything not canned or boxed was a luxury. So much so, I remember the oranges and apples in my Christmas stocking as though they were the finest chocolate candy.

One season I remember vividly, though I can't recall how we got there. Our family was moving from Arkansas to Texas when I was nine, which meant I had to say goodbye to the only best friend I had ever made and gear up for another new school with more new friends . . . again. The drive was hot and depressing. As I stared out the window, I would fixate on the grass against the pavement border as it blurred through city, county, and state lines. And I'd remember the moments with my best friend, Amy, walking to the local pizza barn to share an order of mozzarella sticks before Wednesday night church services or discovering how a sprinkler on her trampoline was the perfect substitution for a big city waterpark in the heat of the summer. And now, Amy was about to be five hours away.

What's worse, upon arrival, I learned that a home or apartment wasn't awaiting us. Our six-person family had no choice but to make a navy blue Econovan our primary residence.

Such a situation would destabilize the worlds of most nine-year-olds, maybe even send them into a panic. And certainly, this was not great news. Details are cloudy as I look back nearly three decades later, but I recall feeling strangely comfortable in that season. Though we didn't have a house, our family was still strong and loving. And something inside of me—call it child's intuition—just knew that joy didn't spring from "things." It bubbled up from a deeper well.

Nine-year-old Candace made an unconscious decision to find happiness in homelessness.

The fold-down bench seat in the back of the van doubled as a bed, and I often counted stars out the window while the others slept. Our dog, a chow-border collie mix named Baby, usually curled up on top of my toes, doubling as an incredible foot warmer.

I loved Baby. I loved dressing her in my clothes and having conversations with her about what I was going to be when I grew up. Baby always listened with a gentle upward glance and blinking eyes as she lay her head atop her folded paws. She walked by my side many afternoons as I hunted for hidden trails in the mysterious world I imagined behind every tree and stone in whatever campground or RV park we had parked. Baby even sat by my side as I unsuccessfully attempted to skip stones on a nearby lake. (I wish I could tell you my skill has improved with age, but sheesh, skipping stones is hard, y'all.)

If I wasn't in deep thought with Baby, I was making an elite city skyline out of newspapers and magazine pages. I folded some of the best skyscrapers you've ever seen. Sprawling giants of iron and stone—at least in my mind. I painted rocks to be the celebrities who would live in my imaginary paper city.

On the rare occasion when it snowed, I'd use cardboard boxes from trash cans or school lunch trays to race down even the shallowest of hills as though I was skiing a double diamond slope in Colorado.

And, no matter where I lay my head to rest at night, I had a Smurfette pillow to substitute for the best friend I had left behind. I tried to reassure Smurfette that one day she'd be old enough to move to her own place away from all those grumpy, blue men. She deserved better. I always had high hopes that Smurfette would become a strong, independent woman, standing tall in her white high heels and a blazer with the puffiest shoulder pads you'd ever seen—possibly because I watched the classic '80s films *Working Girl* and *Big Business* before I should have. (Don't judge. Movie ratings were way different back then.)

I lived in my imagination for nearly a decade. Many grown-ups would consider my fanciful behavior all those years as childish or naïve. They might even accuse me of denial or trying to escape from a reality I wasn't prepared to accept. But, looking back, I think that period actually demonstrates a lesson that many adults would do well to learn:

JOY LIKES TO PLAY.

I love animated films, even as an adult. Sometimes my husband Chris and I spend a date night watching a kids' movie without our children. It doesn't happen often, but every now and then we become the oldest patrons in a theater full of shouting curtain-climbers. (Don't be fooled: Chris isn't a pushover; he's a keeper.)

A couple of years ago, we went to see *Inside Out*. Talk about a great movie. The film glimpses into the brain of a young girl and personifies the primary emotions that exist inside—Anger, Sadness, Fear, Disgust, and, of course, Joy. In the film, Joy is an effervescent girl named—you guessed it—Joy who works hard to see silver linings and stay positive while Anger is brooding, Sadness is sighing, Fear is Fleeing, or Disgust is rolling her eyes. After I watched that film, a question sparked within me: *If the joy we all seek were a real-life person, what would she be like?*

What traits would Joy possess? What would be constant about Joy's character that we might not expect? What surprising personality traits might we discover?

I remember the first time I met Joy. I had seen her cousin, Happiness, show up in snatches of my life as I would laugh at the dinner table while my brother, David, would entertain us with comical stories from his day. (I think he had a personal mission and tally count going under the table to see how many times he could break my dad and cause him to laugh). I remember Happiness as I would sled with my siblings down the biggest snow hill we could find while we lived in a small suburb in Colorado. Happiness had been a longtime friend in my home. She showed herself with every received Christmas wish, every new toy, every laugh while watching our family's favorite sitcoms or blooper home videos shows.

Joy. She was different. Joy was a newfound friend in this new season of leaving a life I loved for a life that seemed uncertain, depressing, and, in all honesty, like a severe setback. Yet, she was surely there in those unsure days. Joy brought me more than a laugh; she granted more than a wish. She offered me contentment, comfort, and peace that I couldn't explain, even when circumstances on the outside didn't look so bright. I didn't meet Joy in a highlight reel moment. I first encountered true joy in an Econovan in an RV park somewhere between Arkansas and Texas.

If Joy were a person and not just an emotion, I bet she'd ask us to play with her. Joy beckons us to a place of carefree laughter, smiles, and peace in the simplest moments. Joy calls us to sniff roses and drink from half-full glasses. Joy skips when others sulk; she takes risks when others cower; she works overtime looking for ways to pierce the darkness with effervescent hope.

The play that Joy offers isn't just for kids, either. We enjoy a good adult coloring book. We reward ourselves with stickers for voting. We ask bank tellers for grape suckers for our "three children" and then enjoy one of them with our two kids. We wish for the dentist to invite us to pick a prize from the treasure chest at the end of our cleaning. I mean, who doesn't want a plastic spider ring or paddle ball? *Especially* after we endure a needle to our gums.

Among the many reasons my video went viral, one that stands out the most is that it gave Joy a voice to cry out, "Take a break and come play!" Many watchers recognized this voice from their own childhood. They had long since abandoned their friend Joy amid life's many letdowns and daily pressures. But when the familiar sound of Joy broke through that screen, they laughed right along with her. Maybe you did, too.

Many nights, like you, I feel the achy void left by Joy's absence when my head hits the pillow. Maybe the money is tight or the bills are bigger than the paychecks, maybe you've been down with a head cold while still needing to take care of two kids under the age of two (both still in diapers, as well), or maybe you lie awake thinking about a future that holds more questions than answers. It's easy to wake up feeling numb and apathetic to Joy's call when you're just hoping to survive the day. When I catch myself in this state, I've learned that it helps to pause and ask a couple of questions to warm up to Joy's playful nature once again:

- What did I do as a child that might spark excitement today?
- What do I wish I could do that I don't make time for?
- What brings me life that I have abandoned because I'm too "old" or "busy" or "dignified?"

Where is Joy calling *me* to play? Maybe it's time to break out the adult coloring book and some crayons, or make some time to sign up for the karaoke night with my sister, or possibly skip the laundry and head to the pool with some bologna, potato chip, and mustard sandwiches, a guilty pleasure I still have to this day, and I'm not sorry.

Nine-year-old Candace didn't stay in that van with her family and dog very long. We eventually moved into that two-star Budget Suites. And then a mobile home. And then a free-standing house. I'm grateful that those days are a faded memory for all of us. They are just a fraction of what our story has become.

At the same time, I'm unashamed of my heritage and example of hard work and perseverance my parents set for me in that lean season. I remember how they taught me to embrace Joy's playful nature. At our leanest moments, my mom would buy a giant bag of Dum-Dum suckers for a mini road trip snack. Dad would fill the tank with ten dollars of gasoline to drive us as far as the fuel would take us, with the windows rolled down and the music cranked up. When we got to our nowhere-and-anywhere destination, we'd take a break, stretch our legs, play a game of tag or hide-and-seek, throw a football, or simply create our own fun. And today, I still carry the lesson I learned: that simple joys can carry us in a significant way.

When times grow rough and uncertain, I hold onto knowing that they'll eventually pass. I'm constructing my own heritage of perseverance for the children that call me "Momma." I work to stay content whether someone is powdering my nose on a television set or I'm just playing with my kiddos on a crumby kitchen floor. I lean on the best partner and friend God could have given me in my husband Chris, knowing that I'm not alone in my attempts to fortify the walls of my home with Joy.

When Chris and I got married more than fifteen years ago, we promised that we would make a point to play with Joy each Christmas. When our family wakes to see what Santa brought, Chris and I step to the side and give each other one toy. It doesn't matter if I got a breast pump or a new cast-iron griddle that year, I knew I was also going to get a toy. One of my favorite memories is when my thoughtful husband gave me a doll that I lost in one of many moves: a Cabbage Patch Kid. (Next is to find that identical Smurfette pillow. She's gotta be out there somewhere!) Chris and I carry on this tradition because we recognize that play is not something that happens *to* you. It's something you choose and pursue. It's something you cultivate. It is something you make space to enjoy. So, we look for opportunities—at Christmastime and all the time—to look for opportunities to play.

One of my favorite marriage memories happened on our ten-year anniversary when we celebrated Christmas in New York City. New York teems with an electric atmosphere of playful discovery and rich history on every crowd-filled street corner. Standing near the base of the ginormous tree in Rockefeller Center, a group of carolers sang the all-too-familiar Christmas hymns and carols that I start listening to in October. (I know some of you just read that and began judging whether you should also listen to Christmas songs three months early. Don't go there. Come back. Stay focused, people.)

As I watched them sing under the sparkling lights, I heard a familiar voice from childhood. A voice that had asked me to build paper skyscrapers and paint rocks, to count stars and explore forests, to talk to Baby and dream about Smurfette's future career in advertising. Standing in Rockefeller Center that day, I heard the call of Joy to come and play.

I looked at my husband and gave him fair warning. "Trust me, Chris. Just trust me."

Slipping up to the side of the crowd, I took my place in the alto section. When the lady next to me gave me the side eye, I whispered that I was a friend of a friend of another friend who had gotten lost on the wrong subway train, but I was so relieved to have finally made it even though I had forgotten my music at my "apartment." She shrugged her shoulders, going along with the joke, albeit grudgingly, and let me share her sheet music. Before I knew it, I was belting out my favorite carols as Chris stood beaming with joy, unable to hide his ever-unimpressed-but-still-so-in-love side smile.

It was a magical moment. Through frosted breath, songs of hope and happiness, and the twinkling lights of all the decorations of "the city that never sleeps," Joy was calling me to play. And despite all the reasons to opt out, I said yes.

Whenever I'm tempted to ignore Joy's call, I think back to that moment and remember what can happen when I say yes to play.

Stop and listen.

Where do you hear the faint call of Joy in your life? Where do you see her waving at you to join the fun? Where do you suspect she's waiting for you? Whether you're living in a van, singing in the middle of Rockefeller Center, or wiping the nose of a sick toddler, our friend Joy is waiting to play.

Say yes. Jump in. And make a memory you won't soon forget.

Joy
STAYS the
COURSE.

Chapter 2

DON'T QUIT YOUR DAYDREAM

As I awoke in my daybed that barely fit within the corners of two walls inside our single-wide trailer home, I fumbled to see what time it was. It was still dark; the rest of my family was fast asleep. I was a freshman in high school, fourteen years old, and my dreams were usually about fitting in, being asked to the dance by the boy I was crushing on, or showing up for final exams naked except for tube socks and sandals borrowed from my dad.

Don't act like you don't know that last one. Or at least pretend that you know it. It will make me feel better.

This dream was different. It had shaken me to my core. No, it wasn't a nightmare . . . but it felt as though somehow I had seen a bit of my destiny wrapped within it. I awoke feeling both clammy and nervous, wondering if I was meant for more than the walls of that trailer home that seemed to bind me in. I made my way to the diminutive, 1980s-inspired shell-shaped sink to splash some water on my face. That's what everyone else seemed to do in the movies when they woke from a dream that shook them to the core . . . so, why not?

I looked at my face in the mirror, staring at the freckles and the acne on each section (as I usually did), but something within insisted I look deeper into my own eyes. That I look at the girl inside the dream I had just dreamed to see if it were possible she was really in there. To my surprise, she was. She was staring right back at me . . . offering hope for the future . . . offering peace . . . offering a quiet confidence that I wasn't hostage to the wood-paneled walls that seemed to suffocate me . . . the kind of confidence that was the result of faith, not arrogance.

So, what kind of dream could impact me so much that I vividly remember it twenty-plus years later? I dreamed my life would one day have a purpose of reaching more people than I could ever count. It was a dream that both fueled me to love people and be intentional about the responsibility that every step I would take in life would lead me to that moment. There were horses and knights and swords and a light-versus-darkness battle, and I had a guitar. Basically, this dream was EPIC. And, even after I woke, I couldn't shake off the feeling that I wanted to live epic, too. I didn't want to drift through life day by day; I wanted to feel the sense of purpose and adventure that was so real in my dream. And, if a guitar had anything to do with that, well, then sign me up.

It would have been easy to shrug off the dream to possible severe heartburn from eating pizza too close to bedtime. (Let's be honest, that was a way more likely reality for my fourteen-year-old self. Heck, it's a common reality at thirty-eight!) Nevertheless, as I stared in the mirror at my inner self, I chose to muster up the faith that my dream could come true someday. I chose to believe it was possible.

Have you ever found your faith wrapped so intrinsically in a dream that you begin to plan your life around it? This was exactly my experience in the days and months following my dream. It did not stop happy-haunting me with hope. And I did something so drastically outside my normal behavior that it left my parents scratching their heads, wondering what had happened to their daughter. For a kid who typically had an elaborate Christmas wish list in the hands of her parents every June, that year I only wrote down one wish: a guitar. I mean, I saw myself playing with skill and confidence in my dream, and so I believed I needed to own one if that was ever going to happen.

Christmas came. We were poor. And that year was especially rough—I was sure I wouldn't get a pricey gift. We were living in a single-wide trailer, testing its capacity limitations by housing three adults, one teenager, and one toddler inside as well as a married couple and two small children on the enclosed porch addition. We were fighting to keep meals on the table that were more than beans and weenies or Hamburger Helper. So, naturally, I didn't get my guitar. I got socks and a roll of hard Life Savers candies in a box shaped like a Santa Christmas train. But, hey, *candy!* I felt disappointment as the rest of the family opened their equally humble gifts. Yet I was warm, happy to be with family, and I actually loved those socks. I felt real joy.

Now I know what you're thinking. What fourteen-year-old loves getting socks for Christmas? But this is one of Joy's beautiful qualities: she is always content with the simplest of things even while she hopes for more. It wasn't the socks for which Joy welled up a fountain of gratitude.

I am not going to lie. All socks are not created equal. Some are way more fun and flirty, and make you feel as though you've stepped into your secret superhero power hidden under your pant leg. I'll give you a second to think of what your super power would be. Me personally? I always choose super speed. I would love to run as fast as the speed of light. Who wouldn't want to outrun a train or a speeding bullet? Who wouldn't want to move so fast that you didn't have to invite the kids to the grocery store run with you? You could just go as soon as you saw something missing and be back home in a flash with the pantry full. You'd avoid the emotional meltdowns as to why you're not going to cave to their sugary cereal requests. And that, my friend, is the main reason (among multiple) why I choose super speed every time.

However, these were not superpower socks. They were white. They were boring. They had one job. Joy didn't jump up and down with immediate enthusiasm at those socks. (Side note: That is why, to this day, you will find me with fun socks that are crazy colors and characters, like tacos and pugs. You should see my collection.)

But in that moment of disappointment, I imagined Joy raising her head to look me square in the eyes from the corner of the room, reminding me of the belonging and safety to be found in the partitions of that trailer home. It's as if she were challenging my disappointment by pointing out that I was no longer homeless—regardless of the size or look of the home—and I was warm and inside that Christmas morning. I had all I needed under that tin roof. I had a family where my parents stayed together through the thick and thin times. I had living examples of what it meant to love someone wholeheartedly without condition. Some of my favorite memories are when my dad would grab my mom's hand and pull her up out of the couch to slow dance to their favorite song while their four children watched and rolled their eyes in embarrassment.

Joy reminded me that a guitar, or even a dream, could never be as special as what I already owned in my family. As I held my white socks and sucked on the red, hard circle candy, I realized my family shared much more than gift-giving; we shared laughs and favorite stories and the goodness of being healthy and together.

And who likes to have cold feet, anyway? Not this girl. I knew that my parents would continue to champion my crazy, dreaming self, even if they didn't get me a guitar. Joy also bubbled up inside me for the warmth I enjoyed, knowing full well what it meant to sleep in the biting cold. Joy stayed the course regardless of past disappointments and was ever present to smile upon the cold, shrink-wrapped plastic value package of plain white crew socks. Joy enabled me to practice gratitude now, even while I hoped for the future when one day I would own and learn to play the guitar of my dreams.

Cleaning up scraps of wrapping paper and silver-thin tinsel that fell off the tree onto the floor, my dad stepped outside. A minute later, he returned with a round-bodied acoustic guitar.

Y'all, it was more than beautiful. It was glorious. It's as if a five-thousand-voice choir began singing Handel's *Messiah* inside my mind. I'll never forget how I felt. I sprang from the floor, wrapped my arms around my daddy's neck, and said the words "thank you" again and again and again. I even let out a few squeals and squeaks of unbelieving happiness and gratefulness as I paused to gather my breath.

I knew the sacrifice my folks had made that year to buy the first puzzle piece of my dream. And that is most certainly what it was. More than a tool to become a songwriter or singer, it was a tangible bridge to the unseen hope that woke me just months earlier. I was determined to learn all I could in every ounce of free time I had. Within the year, I was playing consistently in our church youth worship band. I was learning with and from seasoned musicians who graciously invested in me. I often wonder if it's because they could see my unbridled passion for the instrument or if they could see the dream in me. Regardless, whether in the shivering cold or sweltering heat of the front porch where I would practice daily, I knew it was tied to my destiny. All because of a dream at fourteen.

Maybe you've not had a dream in the middle of the night that woke you in a cold sweat. But you've had walking daydreams and visions of something that calls to you: a task, a talent, a desire to do good, a hope for more than your circumstances dictate. I would love to tell you that I didn't have to wait to see my dream come true in the daylight and that I found the fast track to all I was hoping for. I can't. Even now, I know there are still parts of that dream that anticipate being lived out.

Waiting is a fickle thing. It has a way of making dreams fade from vibrant color to washed-out gray, reducing them to once-upon-a-time wishes. Thankfully, there's a friend in the waiting that we too often ignore. Something I've since learned about Joy is that she prompts us to hope.

Have you seen the movie *The Santa Clause*? In it there's a scene where one of the characters is discussing when he stopped believing in Santa. You'd think his disbelief would have begun by rumors spread by other children in the halls at elementary school. But no. He says, "I was three. All I wanted was an Oscar Meyer weenie whistle. Christmas came. No weenie whistle." The dialogue is funny, because, well, who gives up on their belief in Santa as a three-year-old? Apparently, this boy's disappointment about not getting a weenie whistle fueled his lack of faith and joy. Every Christmas since then, he would refuse to join the holiday fun or enjoy the season. I often think of this scene when I am in a season of waiting for dreams to come true. Each year the dream is deferred, I have a choice to believe what I feel in my heart is true or allow my hope and the dream to die. There's beauty in facing adversity and disappointment while we wait that develops a deeper faith in what we're longing for . . . *if* we embrace the fact that joy indeed always hopes and stays the course.

We all want joy; we all want to live lives filled to the brim and overflowing with it in every second. But what we fail to realize is we can't have genuine joy without hope. When you have nothing to anchor your future dreams, desires, or visions to, you become more cynical and less joyful. Here's a mystery I am discovering: If I am not actively believing in hope, I cannot experience joy. Hope is like a muscle—it takes practice to believe it and live it out. It takes a willful decision to hope in an unseen future. I honestly believe that when times are the toughest, it's when we need joy the most.

But can I just say that you'll never truly experience joy in the bleakest of circumstances if you resign to believing your circumstance will never get better. Please don't be so quick to move past this thought. How we respond to life when it doesn't match our expectations will determine how much we experience a life full of joy. I have found the secret sauce to joy is holding onto hope and faith that my situation will most certainly get better even if it gets worse. The more I persevere in hope when obstacles threaten the life of my dreams, the more joy I experience in the journey, especially in the waiting. Certainly, there will be obstacles. Surely, there will be detours. Definitively, there will be struggle. But any dream that makes you come alive is a dream worth fighting for with hope.

I could waste all my days worried if my dreams will come true or disappointed when they don't. Or I could resist the urge to cave beneath my circumstance and defiantly stay the course with joy in each step, each disappointment, each moment that offers me crew socks instead of destiny. Hope is the reason Joy stays the course.

Listen, I don't know what dreams and visions motivate you. I do know this: Although dreams come quickly in the night, they tend to take days, weeks, months, years, and even sometimes decades to realize. I have found that Joy is a friend like no other in the waiting. She doesn't let you forget to see the forest for the trees when you're in the thick of it. She keeps calling you to play on the trails full of haze and fog when you can't see clear steps ahead. She keeps moving toward the dream with unapologetic hope and confidence that one day you'll find a clearing and your dream will meet you there. If you haven't heard someone encourage you in a while, let me be the first to say:

DON'T QUIT YOUR DAYDREAM.

STAY THE COURSE.

Find and hold on to simple joys as breadcrumbs leading you to where you belong.

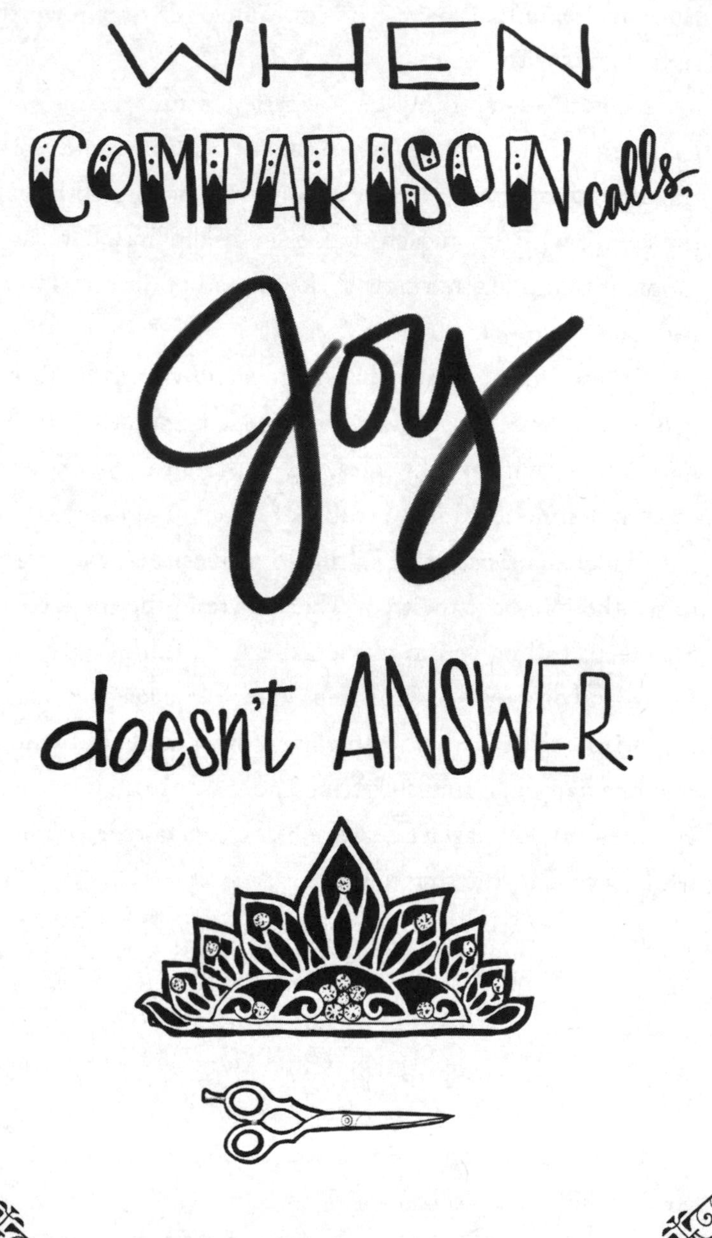
WHEN
COMPARISON calls,
Joy
doesn't ANSWER.

Chapter 3

UH-OH, JOY HAS A FRENEMY

I had hustled my daydream so furiously that I found myself packing boxes of picture frames with photos of family and friends to relocate to a college dorm room. I had auditioned for and received a music scholarship to a relatively small private university four hours from home, and was grateful for the new adventure of trading wood-paneled walls for white cinder block ones.

I was standing on the edge of my coming-of-age story, about to live away from my parents' protection, schedule, and house rules for the first time. Hello, Cheetos to be eaten in bed, Waffle House runs at 2:00 a.m., and cold pizza for breakfast whenever I wanted! (Oh, sweet college, eighteen-year-old freedom!) I was a new kid on the block. And so was every other college freshman, of course. However, I couldn't see that. I had lived in so many homes and been the new kid so many times that I assumed showing up at college would be no different.

Only this time, instead of showing up with a fresh shot at making friends, I instantly felt as though I didn't fit in. I was comfortable being all the labels I had worked so hard to be called in high school. Not a single person knew me by any label, talent, or ability as I walked this strange new campus. I felt like my coming-of-age story was about to nosedive fast, and I became desperate to avoid that.

I remember sitting outside at a small circle of brick benches in the middle of campus comparing myself to the others who passed by. I promptly knew I wasn't going to rival the beauty pageant queens, nor the scholarly bookworms who made me feel as though I had reverted to kindergarten reading level just hearing them speak. And after attending my first classes with music and theater majors, I realized my singing, acting, and guitar playing were no match for the vast talent pool surrounding me. I was both enamored by the number of beautiful, talented, well-put-together eighteen-year-olds and scared to death of them.

For the first time, I didn't know where I fit in. Or even if I would ever fit in. So I decided to implement my most fail-proof plan, the one that had always worked in times past: make 'em laugh.

Over the next couple of years, it wouldn't be odd to find me pulling pranks, trying my hand at stand-up comedy, doing Chris Farley impersonations in the cafeteria, or writing songs based on crazy real-life experiences—like that time I suffered a squirrel attack in my hair.

I know. I just said an odd phrase that made your brain

pause. Let me explain. When I was sixteen, I was attacked by a squirrel that jumped from a telephone pole to impressively land atop my head. Yes, you read that right. I ran about half a block with it stuck inside my ginormous "Texas hair" before I gained enough gumption to slap it off my head toward the ground. It was a horrific experience (for the squirrel too!), but it made for great song material—and I'm not one to let that go to waste.

Anywho. I became the life of the party and felt responsible to maintain the title. It was my new identity. I was "the fun." Yes, it was fun for a season as I felt the attention and laughs from people with whom I knew I could never compare in any other category. But, man. Quickly, the fun began to fizzle. I remember one night feeling the slow burn at both ends of trying to be someone and something I wasn't . . . *all* the time. Unfortunately, that one night could have been much more devastating than it actually is today as I look back to recall its events.

Leaves were falling and flooding the beautiful campus with bright hues of green, orange, red, and yellow. Football season was in progress, and homecoming was imminent. I was a part of a national theater fraternity, and our small theater wanted to nominate someone to represent our chapter for the honor of homecoming queen. When no one immediately stepped up, I had the idea it would be comical for me, the plus-size wonder, to be presented next to a couple of size-zero reigning pageant queens. It was like the opening scene in the first *Hunger Games* movie. "I volunteer," I said as

I stood to my feet. I remember my friend's reply, "Yes! That'd be hilarious! Let's have Candace do it!"

Just like that, I was the nominee for homecoming queen. No worries, I thought. It wasn't like I was competing in a beauty pageant. I didn't have to practice an opening dance number or do grueling interviews to which my standard reply would be "world peace." I merely had to show up in a dress two times: on the day that the student body voted and on the football field the day they'd announce who won.

So, I went to a couple of meetings where we were instructed where to stand and walk as they announced our names. But once again, I was sizing up the room, playing my constant comparison game. The problem is that when you play Comparison's game, you always end up as the loser. As I looked around the room, I was one of the few people who weighed more than two hundred pounds, didn't know the first thing about applying eyeliner, and was more concerned with how many tacos I was going to eat after the meeting was over. The day the student body voted, I borrowed a dress that fit me well. I had been a size 22 in women's clothing when the semester started and now wore a size 18 thanks to a new prescribed weight-loss drug I was taking.

Yeah. Comparison had such a grip on me that I had seen my family doctor during the summer break and asked for a pill to help me be thinner . . . and hopefully prettier and more lovable in the process. At the time, I thought this drug could be my golden ticket. But it was so "wonderful" that it is no longer even prescribed. Apparently, one side effect was lowering serotonin in the brain, the neurotransmitter that is popularly thought to contribute to feelings of well-being. I was unaware that I was chemically conditioning myself for depression.

I stood backstage waiting for my name to be called, hoping my dress would inspire half the male student body to want to marry me . . . or at least make out with me. (At our school we jokingly boasted about females getting a "ring by spring or your money back" and being more concerned with getting an "M.R.S. degree" than finding and developing ourselves.) One such guy, a crush I developed in our mutual music classes, was also backstage. Well, wouldn't you know it? This guy came over and offered the most "endearing" compliment every woman wants to hear: "You don't look at all like Chris Farley when you dress up."

Wait. What? Did he just say that out loud? If you don't know who Chris Farley is, get on Google ASAP, and you'll see why I spent the next few moments trying to act as though I wasn't devastated and searching for a funny, stinging, quick-witted comeback. The joke never came. Instead, my name was called. So, I put on my "everything's fine" mask and acted as though all was well. But it wasn't. I just wanted to cry. You'd have never known as I walked across the platform that my heart was broken and I felt undesirable in every way. I smiled, put on dramatic poses, said something sarcastic, I'm sure, and hid the hurt behind a smile.

The big reveal of homecoming queen contest winner was still a few days away. In the meantime, I stewed on the backhanded compliment spewed haphazardly by an honest college guy.

I don't know if you've ever been there. You know, when you're faking it until you're making it? When you're trying to make a dazzling first impression. Or laughing along with someone else's inside joke that you don't actually understand. Or maybe when you're pasting on a smile in public even when you feel like you're barely holding it together. Well, I was there. And I was not happy. Can I take a moment to be honest about Joy's role in my personal life at that moment? Well, let's just say she was an unattainable superstar with whom I pretended to be best friends. I'd act like we were intimate friends, like she was the source of all my rollicking good fun, but it was just that: *an act*. Joy was nowhere to be found when the crowds were gone. And, slowly, I couldn't even see her in the crowds and "fun" either. Within short months, rapidly, she was becoming all but a distant memory.

The "fun" was in full force, sure, but it was empty without Joy.

For the first time in all my life, I regretted being the fun. I wanted desperately to be the pretty one. The alluring one. The one who took your breath away with stunning beauty. I was blinded by the need to be anyone or anything other than myself. And I would have traded places with anyone else at that time, any other contestant, no questions asked. In the isolation of my self-disappointments, I did what I did best: laugh it off. Hiding behind jokes at the expense of my self-esteem, I found myself callously ignoring the voice of Joy and my authentic self and embracing this new judgmental friend, Comparison.

Oh boy. Comparison is so pretty on the outside. She would whisper thoughts about who I should and could become (even if it meant turning my back on my authentic self). And she was incredibly persuasive. But Comparison wasn't a friend of Joy at all. She was the ultimate frenemy of Joy. Her intentions weren't fueled by the same inspiration that Joy offered. Comparison said I wasn't enough unless I was like those I admired. She filled me with jealousy and cynicism. She was the mean girl, snarky and coldhearted. She only felt good about herself when she was putting others down. Regardless, I gave her ample opportunity to speak lies to me of my worth and value. I think we've all been there, if you're not there right now. When Joy seems a distant or frivolous indulgence, Comparison promises a "high," a happy feeling of self-worth (albeit fleeting) when we're on the winning side of the unspoken competition.

Oh well. The show must go on. That's what they tell you in theater, and that's what I believed. No matter what was happening internally, the day of the homecoming queen announcement had arrived. I woke up that Saturday to have brunch with my family who had come to town. My dad was there to walk me onto the football field, stand with me, and smile as they awarded various titles to all the other beautiful girls . . . but definitely not to me. I felt bad that my parents were taking this college prank a bit more seriously than I was and had driven four hours to support me with their hard-earned gas money. So, I knew I better do my best to keep faking the role I had embraced. I remember applying makeup that morning, wearing a garter belt to help me suck it in, and even slipping my feet into unfamiliar pumps. (Listen, y'all. Pumps would have to do. To this day, it pains me to wear a pair of heels for more than a consecutive thirty-six minutes. The struggle is real.)

As I stood sinking into the plush grass, arms locked with my dad, names began rolling thunderously over the football stadium speakers, followed by raucous cheers from the stands and sweet flower bouquets delivered to beautiful young women. Upon hearing the name of the second runner-up, I tuned out the boisterous speakers. After all, that was the highest honor I could see obtaining. I began shifting attention to my friends and family in the stands waving and making silly faces back and forth. Abruptly, my dad interrupted me with a sharp elbow to the ribs. "Hey, come on! Let's go up there. They called your name." I eyeballed him like he must've heard wrong. Surely they didn't call *my* name. However, I looked across the field to see ceremony officials walking toward me. Before I could collect the reality of what was happening, I had a sash around my shoulder, the biggest bouquet of flowers I had ever been handed resting in my arms like a swaddled infant Jesus, and a tiara on my head. A tiara, y'all. I was ushered, like the President of the United States in a volatile situation, to a homecoming flatbed trailer to take a seat of honor for the second half. To this day, I have no clue if our team won the game. My head was swirling with thoughts, none of which I am proud to admit to you as you read this. Instead of embracing the joy of the moment, I remember feeling this overwhelming disconnect from the love everyone was showing me. I felt their cheers were in fact masqueraded jeers. I had become my own worst joke. And everyone affirmed it by making me their queen.

I made it through the next week with fraudulent smiles of appreciation, doing everything I could do for a laugh with my new elected title of "Homecoming Queen." I stored my tiara in a red-velvet-lined wooden box and made "queenly visits" to the other girls in my dorm in the late night/early morning hours, wearing a see-through dress (exposing a sparkly bra and panties underneath) and the crown on my head. I had no filter. I was certain this was the kind of queen they had voted for—the object of the joke. (Which it wasn't! These people genuinely loved me. All of me. Whether I could make them laugh or not.) I was immensely honored by my friends, yet Comparison kept whispering within that I was a nothing and a nobody without making them all laugh. I was so sure of this in my mind that only a week later I found myself at my weakest point.

I cannot explain how I spun out of control so quickly other than I had a complete lack of clarity in seeing reality for what it was. I had created this false narrative that I was the punchline to everyone's joke. And I was quickly realizing I couldn't spend the rest of my days in that role. One way or another, I was going to make certain of that.

One night I was atypically alone in my very socially

active dorm room. In the strange stillness, I indulged every ill thought I ever had about myself in comparison to everything I longingly wanted to impossibly become. I counted all the things I felt were wrong about me, and I did not hold back. I said things to myself that night that I would never even dream of saying to another person, they were so heartless. But that's how worthless I felt. Then I rushed to the conclusion that I wanted the laughing at me to end. And, in haste, the only way I could see making that reality was ending my own life. I pulled out a sharp pair of kitchen scissors from my desk.

Through streaming tears and what I can only describe as the darkest thoughts I have ever given action to, I began to cut myself before one of my best friends and roommates found me. I was broken and ashamed of who I was in front of her. I felt exposed behind the cracked smile. I was reduced to emotional rubble. But she didn't shame me.

With slow-fading shock, she helped me bandage my wounds, wiped my tears, replaced words of life covering the dark words of death I had embraced, helped me call my mother to tell her what was really going on and ask for help, and flushed the remaining weight-loss pills. After a couple hours, we walked the campus together in what was, by then, the middle of the night. I remember being silent. I remember her being silent as well. Not a single word needed to be spoken. Instead, I looked at my frosted breath as I exhaled . . . and very slowly, evaporating puff of air by evaporating puff, I became grateful. Overwhelmingly grateful I was still breathing. Grateful my friend found me and stopped me. Grateful to be alive. Grateful to just be me. Suddenly, the desire to be anyone or anything else other than me didn't hold a candle to the fact that I was alive and given another chance. Under my very concerned and wise mother's orders, I saw a therapist and began to take medicine for a short while to regulate the serotonin levels in my brain.

Comparison is deadly dangerous. Most of my friends from college may be shocked to know just how lonely and desperate for attention, acceptance, and love that I felt in that season because I was too busy wearing a mask of comedic contentment. Ironically, I was alone. I was unhappy. Despite my outward displays, I believed I wasn't enough.

Enough. That one little word packs a brutal punch, doesn't it? Because every time we say to ourselves that we're not good enough, pretty enough, smart enough, or (fill in the blank) enough, we're reinforcing the lie that our worth is based on someone else's standard, a standard of which we fall short. It drives me nuts. Bonkers. I know what it's like to never feel pretty enough. To never feel smart enough. To not feel talented enough. To not feel athletic enough. To just downright feel . . . NOT ENOUGH. When did we forget that we're *all* amateurs at this thing called life? Give yourself permission to be just that. We're all in process. We're all stumbling around trying our best to get it right, and at times, failing spectacularly. So let's take the pressure off ourselves and others, quit with the enoughs, and give each other some grace. I rarely say that I know something for sure, but I do know that every single time that I don't feel enough . . . that feeling, friends, is not joy.

You see, when Comparison calls, Joy doesn't answer the phone. I cannot tell you just how many times I was empty of joy (genuine joy) from my life because I was too busy comparing myself to others. When we compare, ultimately we fall short somewhere. Joy knows this. That's why she doesn't even entertain the thought.

Y'all. Think of it this way. If Joy had a smartphone, she would put it on silent when she saw the ocean waves hit the shore instead of scrolling through her phone to see what her friends were doing in that moment, and then feeling left out or less than. That's what her frenemy, Comparison, would do. But Joy puts her phone away to be fully present and content where she is; to play in the sand, breathe in the ocean air, and count the colors that cascade over the horizon while hiding that secret moment in her heart. No matter the trial or triumph, I find it's easier to silence the calls of Comparison when we are content with our lives. Contentment is the antidote to Comparison. Because while Comparison sets its sights on what it does not have, Contentment anchors itself in the gift of the present. That's where we find our Joy.

The day that I posted the video of myself enjoying a birthday toy, I had no desire to be a record setter or record breaker. I was content in being a stay-at-home momma and living an anonymous life, content with running errands and taking a small moment to relish a simple joy. My intentions merely were to share a moment between momma friends, not to be the next viral internetwebs star. If you've seen the video, you know Comparison wasn't anywhere to be seen in that car.

Now, since the video went viral and I've been handed opportunity upon opportunity to change the trajectory of not only *my* life but my *family's* lives, people have said some of the most encouraging and kind words. And some have said some downright awful things. Interestingly, the encouragers and critics share two similar responses.

On one hand, I have heard it said that I haven't deserved any of this. Listen, I get it. It's a four-minute video, nearly three minutes of which is nothing but laughter. Yet there's this unspoken comparison being placed on my life when such criticism comes: a stay-at-home mom doesn't have much value. But in my humble opinion, if something wonderful happens to a person of little societal value (whether you buy into that opinion or not), shouldn't we rejoice and champion those moments? Ironically, the flip side compliment ("It couldn't happen to a better person," or "No one I know deserves this more than you") doesn't sit well with me either because it, too, is that old, familiar voice of Comparison. There's an unspoken rule that advertises you have to be deserving, worthy, and merited to have joy (you have to be "enough"). Since when? When did we start accepting this as the norm? Well, I sure don't know, but I do know Joy doesn't tolerate that nonsense. Joy does not discriminate. She is a friend to any and all who would receive her.

I had to learn the hard way that laughing it off is no joke.

It's no joke to tell yourself you're not enough and then go out and act like it. Because the truth is you *are* enough, and there is a better way. As it turns out, Chewie had the right idea all along—he laughed it *up*.

Joy longs to take the good and the bad days alike and find space to laugh it up, embracing life to the fullest, come what may. Comparison calls just to tell us we're not enough, and we tend to want to laugh it off, putting on a brave face and a pretend smile, hiding our hurt behind a mask.

I don't know what you're internalizing as you read this chapter. You could question that I didn't even have a genuine reason to spiral out of control to the point of suicide because you've experienced much darker and more dreadful external circumstances. You could be feeling sorry for me and think how that would never happen to you . . . that you would've handled it differently . . . that you may have managed your emotions with much more tact, wisdom, and grace. Can I challenge you—as a friend—to pause here? If you've agreed with either side of those responses, the voice of Comparison may be louder in your mind than you give it credence.

You are worthy of joy, and no one can take that away from you. You don't have to earn it. Shut out the shouts of Comparison. Joy refuses to entertain the conversation, and so should you.

Joy
EVICTS
shame.

Chapter 4

WHEN GOD PLAYS MATCHMAKER

I remember the moment that I felt unworthy of true love. I had spent most of my teenage years and adult life trying to erase that moment from my memory. Yet it's worth identifying. It's worth calling to the forefront and naming it for what it is so that it does not, cannot, and will not hold my joy hostage on any level. So, I vulnerably share a moment that shifted and shaped the course of my relationships from that day forward.

I was a husky, freckled thirteen-year-old girl with high hopes of falling in love and sharing my first kiss with a boy who had the voice of Sean Connery, the eyes of Kurt Russell, and the snarky, rebellious attitude of Christian Slater. I know, I know. I have just dated myself terribly. What can I say? Those were the actors in all the romantic comedies I would rent from the local video store on VHS to watch alone in my room while eating a bucket of microwave popcorn and cinnamon gummy candies.

They were also the actors in the pics and posters of my preteen magazines that I'd tear out and tape to my bedroom walls. The Christian Slater poster was proudly displayed over my nightstand that housed my modern, neon, see-through phone that lit up when it rang. If you had that phone, you were a baller, shot caller. Not that I fully understand that phrase, but I am a mom who frequently tries out slang about twenty years from its conception. I was barely a teenager, with an array of stuffed animals on my bed, but that didn't stop me from daydreaming about meeting my very own real-life version of Christian Slater. I kept waiting and waiting for what seemed like forever to share my first kiss with the boy of my dreams.

Suddenly, I found myself being noticed and appreciated by a young man at church only a few months older than me. He was cute . . . enough. Let's be honest. In seventh grade, it's hard to be acne- and awkward-free in every area of physical appearance. He was no dreamboat, but he was affectionate toward me. As a matter of fact, he was the first peer to take an interest in me. We spent weeks calling ourselves boyfriend and girlfriend and telling others we were "going out." We had held hands in the backseat of a car, so I knew the next inevitable step was that glorious first kiss.

One Wednesday night at church, he asked me if I wanted to skip the service for our age group. It was dangerous and rebellious, yes. But I knew it might just be the moment I would finally step into my dreams of being loved like the beautiful lead in the romantic comedies I would watch every weekend. I took his hand as he passed from one darkened room to the next, jiggling each door handle to see if it was locked or unlocked. We found a room with no lights, walked inside, closed and locked the door behind us, and stepped into a dark corner.

I remember wearing a V-neck brown shirt with tiny, white flowers and an ill-fitting pair of jeans. Clearly, I was poorly dressed for this momentous occasion. It wasn't at all what I had been watching or dreaming about, and I knew it. But in that moment, I also doubted that I would ever find someone to love me or look at me like this boy looked at me, so I continued to follow what I assumed to be his experienced lead.

He began kissing me, and it was awful. It definitely was *not* what I had dreamed about, and I began to feel uncomfortable.

I asked him to stop and told him we should get back to the group, but he wouldn't stop. I was trapped in the dark corner that at first had allured me figuratively and then, very literally. And what started as an innocent desire to share a first kiss ended with sexual assault.

To be honest, I don't remember much during those next moments except my own hushed cries for him to stop. But my cries went unheard. He told me if we went back to the group now, I would be in trouble for not being where my parents trusted I was supposed to be. Then, I had the overwhelming fear of trying to explain everything that happened in that dark corner to my mom and dad.

I avoided eye contact with my family for weeks afterward, my thoughts and emotions leaving me feeling dirty, exposed, and violated—innocence lost. I couldn't look this young man in the eyes, either. I broke up with him and avoided him at every pass. But unfortunately, I also developed a fractured way of thinking, telling myself I wasn't worthy of true love. I started to believe what happened in that shadowy corner was solely my fault because it was what I deserved. Even more damaging, I began to replicate that behavior in most every opposite-sex relationship. Kissing would never end at kissing. I subconsciously believed I would never be fully loved unless I satisfied the physical desires of the boys I was dating. And, well, that's putting it mildly. Paralyzed by a fear that I was unlovable without performance, I gave away my purity (really, I gave away my power) without ever finding the one thing I wanted most: someone to love me unconditionally.

The lowest moment for me came at a college party where I found myself on my knees in a damp, dimmed bathroom performing for a guy who, to this day, remains nameless. I knew even then that was not what I wanted. What I wanted, ached for, was for someone to hold me and kiss me as someone loved. But, that's not what happened . . . at all. I pulled myself off the floor and drove back to my college dorm room with a feeling of regret that I couldn't shake. Eventually, my lack of self-worth turned into a much graver thing: for the very first time, I knew Shame.

At some point, I would try to evict this ugly monster.

Nearing the end of my time in college, shortly after attempting suicide, I clearly could see I'd hit rock bottom. I didn't love who I was. I didn't feel loved. And I was doubtful I would ever find true love that was kind and unselfish. To make matters worse, I had a record. I gave in to the voice that enticed me to perform for acceptance. I performed for laughs from the crowd. I performed in relationships that were frail and fleeting, destined to fail. And then, this same voice wooing me to perform would change its tone the moment I did, becoming an internal accuser of how unlovable and worthless I was because I had caved. Shame is a big, nasty bully, y'all. In a rare moment of clarity, I knew I needed to release its grip over my thoughts and actions, but had no clue how. So, I did what I knew best. I began performing in a different way. I would attempt to play the role of a good, Christian, church girl.

I started working part-time at a church that had an end-of-summer back-to-school bash open to the entire community. The event was my first opportunity to meet the group I'd be leading and working alongside. The parking lot overflowed with bounce houses, a rock-climbing wall, over two hundred teenagers and young adults, and loud music from a portable sound system. I parked in one of the spaces reserved for visitors and was greeted by smile after smile of volunteers. The people were all seemingly good people, warm and genuine in their introductions.

When I met *him*, though, I had no idea he would be so extraordinary to my everyday life for the rest of my days.

Chris Payne was soft-spoken yet spunky. He had long, brown hair with bright red-dyed streaks and a long goatee that was rubber-banded into an even longer spike beneath his chin—not the typical volunteer you'd expect to see around teenage students in a church environment. He was rough around the edges, to say the very least. He loved tattoos, motorcycles, entertainment television wrestling, and his newly found relationship with God. We shook hands cordially, and he told me his name. At the moment, I didn't think much of that chance meeting until a few months later when God began to play matchmaker as only God can.

Chris was not only edgy but a very skilled drummer as well, so we had music in common. Being only two years apart in age, we also were in the same small group of young adults invited to scheduled socials ranging from ice cream runs after church to the local high school's Friday night football game. Except that over the course of three or four months, we were the only people who showed up. We'd make small talk for a while, but inevitably there were many awkward silences as we sat searching for common interests other than music and movie quotes. Although, that's a great foundation, if I'm being honest.

One Wednesday night, however, in an unlikely turn of events, several other people joined us at a local late-night hangout that served ice cream, corn dogs, mozzarella sticks, and all sorts of Southern-fried comforts. I could sense the relief in the air that we didn't have to be alone. We mingled with our circles of friends until slowly, one by one, everyone started to leave, and our small, separate circles condensed into one. Chris regularly jumped into the conversation with wit and humor and sarcasm. *Hmmm, this is different*, I thought to myself, seeing him casually come alive, all of a sudden very cool. As the crowd diminished further, we found ourselves the last ones in the parking lot, but this time being alone was different. We sat on the tailgate of his Texas pick-up, the restaurant's bright neon sign beaming over us as our conversation went from laughter to deeper topics. I don't even know how or when the atmosphere changed as we talked, but it did. That night, we went from polite strangers who rarely exchanged two words to discussing our hopes and dreams for the future.

Suddenly, not only was I interested in getting to know all I could know about him, but I was enthralled by every word he shared. Before we were aware, time had stolen the night as we sat dispensing our life stories, failures, and dreams long after the restaurant had closed and everyone had gone home. It was 4:00 a.m., and the sun was about to rise any moment. Surely, a new day dawned along with a new light that shined on a promising friendship. Chris was quite different than I previously supposed, and certainly not the "type" of guy I had usually gravitated toward. Every girl, at some point, makes a list of the qualities and traits she wants in a lifelong partner. If I went line by line on my list, Chris would be the exact physical opposite of my dream man. Yet he possessed character traits on my list that were hard to deny. I could see he was kind, authentic, and full of integrity. And he oozed humility, a trait never experienced at such a level with my traditional, theater, performance-based crowd. To simply put it, Chris was unassuming. And I was a fan.

A few weeks passed, and we began to gladly spend time outside of the dates only God could have set up. Chris would come to my house after his day job, a thirty-minute-out-of-the-way drive, just for an opportunity to check in on me. I'd love to say that he was intentionally pursuing me through the lens of a man who loved a woman. He wasn't. He was being a friend. He was cheering me on in my passions. He was meeting and embracing my family as his own and, in the process, becoming my best friend. *I*, however, was secretly falling madly in love with him. Throughout all these encounters, there wasn't an ounce of flirtatious behavior from him. He was consistently kind and generous, but I also knew he was like this with everyone. That's just who he was. Chris was hard to read, y'all. To be honest, he still is to this very day. But it didn't keep me from hoping.

My hopes would turn into reality one night when we were casually hanging out at my parents' home watching a movie. As the film came to an end, one of us said something that incited a playful soft punch to the arm. Within minutes, we were playfully wrestling, and then came the "serious pause." You know the "serious pause," right? The one where the whole world stops and you gaze into each other's eyes. In that pause your eyes begin saying every single thought of secret romance you've ever thought about the person while bouncing back and forth like a championship ping-pong game. Without ever saying a word, I was longingly speaking all my hopes and fears while I looked into Chris's eyes. What's more, I felt like he heard me.

To my surprise, I could read his eyes as well. I read the story of a man who was afraid to fall in love but who would never take his heart back once he offered it. Yeah, that "serious pause." In that moment, I felt as if we were two people seeing each other for who we truly are. Gazing into eyes swiftly became kissing on the lips. We then became insanely aware that it was late, we were alone, and we were crazy about each other. We paused the hot, steamy action and leapt to our feet. I'll never forget how he caressed my face and kissed my forehead. "I've got to go. But I'll see you tomorrow, right?" I walked him to the front door, he kissed me goodnight, and I could barely sleep because I couldn't stop thinking about him.

It was only three weeks from that moment that Chris asked me to promise to marry him. (Yes, you read that right. *Three weeks!*) The man was nothing I thought I wanted but everything I knew I needed. To quote one of my favorite movies, *When Harry Met Sally*: "When you realize you want to spend the rest of your life with somebody, you want the rest of your life to start as soon as possible." We found ourselves confessing quite quickly our feelings for one another.

The most incredible thing about my guy is how he restored joy to me, replacing my shame. While Chris pursued me during our engagement with a pure love I had never known, he would tell me how beautiful I was. He'd open doors for me. He'd call in the middle of the day to say he was thinking about me. He'd write me love notes. He'd unashamedly clutch my hand as we walked. He'd gaze at me while we shared a meal as though all time had frozen. Simply put, Chris did something I had never done for myself: He respected me. When I would find myself inclined to repeat past physical behaviors, he'd intentionally pause, redirect the moment, and only hug me. He would hold me without expectation of sexual satisfaction. Instead, he would wrap me in his arms, hold me to his chest, and let the silence of just being together be enough.

If we were to share our future, and I hoped we would, then I wanted to tell him my past. He loved me so well I felt safe enough to do that. So, one day, I laid everything bare that I could remember . . . all of it. It wasn't pretty. I wasn't proud of it. And more than anything, I hoped my past wouldn't scare off the man I had come to love.

Chris listened patiently, and when I had said everything I needed to say, he reassured me that I was exactly what he wanted. He didn't even miss a beat. He told me he loved me regardless of any past encounters and that his promise to marry me didn't hinge on anything I could do for him but solely on the merit that he knew me and loved me for me. Chris began disrupting the atmosphere of shame I felt as he spoke joy to my thirsty soul. For the first time, I was fully known and fully loved. I dare say, that is one of life's greatest joys we will ever experience.

Within a year of sharing our first kiss, we were married.

Yes, within ten months, we were sharing a different kiss at an altar in front of our families and friends, declaring our loyalties and vows never to leave and always to love. This love was unlike any other I had ever felt. I knew he loved me for who I was, not what I could do for him or what he could get from me. Chris restored my faith that a man could be kind and gave me hope that I could be lovable.

We got married at Christmastime on the Riverwalk in San Antonio, Texas. Christmas twinkling lights were strung in the trees lining the river. I carried a fragrant bouquet of stargazer lilies and rich, red roses. It was a crisp, cool evening. My dad walked me over the bridge to a beautiful landing where we said our vows, cried a few tears as we felt the gravity of the covenant we were making, held hands, and locked eyes with every glance. It was an intimate service in every sense of the word, the same intimacy I had craved as a seventh-grade, freckled, wishful girl. The feeling wasn't lost on me.

However, like any good love story, conflict entered the scene. When our honeymoon ended, I couldn't shake the deep-down sense that I didn't deserve Chris, or that maybe he didn't deserve me. The harmful thoughts and habits in my heart ran deep.

We all have these moments in life when something or someone tries to steal our joy. In such times, Shame comes knocking on the door and barges in on the happy home Joy has created.

Have you ever had a horrible roommate? I'm not talking about one who forgets to do the dishes now and then or doesn't remember trash day. I'm speaking about the kind of roommate who steals from you, rummages through your underwear drawer, borrows clothes without asking, or reads your diary only to recite the pages aloud in future conversations while mocking your deepest hopes and dreams. Have you ever tried to live peacefully with someone who never wants peace?

When we allow Shame to move in with Joy, this is the internal struggle we endure. Shame is a thief. He robs us of our identity and our destiny and replaces them with myths that we are not worth any good that may come our way. Shame is the roommate that always bullies, always argues, never takes accountability for truth, never trusts, keeps poorly mismanaged records of wrongs, and always fights to claim ownership without paying the rent. We've all had Shame knock on the door of our hearts and minds. No one is perfect. No one lives an entirely blameless life. But the truth is Shame and Joy cannot ever live peacefully together. We must choose one. And all too often, we opt to put up with Shame's shenanigans instead of staying the course with Joy.

But like any journey worth making, saying goodbye to Shame is a process, with many ups and downs. Shame had so long been a part of my life that I had a lot of unlearning to do, and sometimes I still got stuck.

One night, in stark contrast to the moments of euphoric honeymoon bliss we had shared in our tiny apartment, the struggle between Joy and Shame brewed and bubbled inside me until it finally erupted like a volcano of toxic emotion and unfair accusation toward my husband. Suspicious of Chris's love because I couldn't understand it, I spewed words of doubt and disbelief. I remember saying things like: "How can you love someone like me?" "You don't really love me; you love the idea of marriage more than me." "You're just pretending to be a good man, but one day you'll show me you're no better than any other guy. You'll only want me for what you can get and leave me when you don't get it."

(Let's just chalk this up to being not one of my finest moments, okay? Okay.)

Even as I write this memory for you to read, I imagine Shame feeling the push of Joy having taken over the apartment, and Shame was pushing back. He'd have to wait now as Joy would spring into the shower every morning while he stood with his towel and toiletries in hand. I could envision Joy lighting deliciously scented candles at the end of the day, the kind Shame always hated. She would take the last piece of cake in the fridge (it was hers, after all), the coveted recliner, and, to top it all off, the remote control. Shame was hacked off.

Now, here's what is remarkable about Mr. Chris Payne: He stayed. He proved my worst fears wrong. He put to rest every lie and accusation I hurled in his direction. He reassured. He continued to love and offer hope that I may seriously be lovable. His resilient joy was wrangling and contending for me long after I had given up the fight for myself. And he inspired me to do what I knew I needed to do on my own. Because as stubborn a scrapper as this man I love is, Chris could only fight the battle for my heart from the outside. He couldn't be the only dog in the fight. I had to embrace Joy myself, and own the decision to evict Shame for good. Ultimately, I had to be the one to give Joy full right to occupy every part of my present, every longing for my future, and every disgrace from my past.

There is nothing in me that believes it's easy being on the offense to reacquire spaces in your heart and mind that Shame has stolen. I'd be an utter fool and lie to you if I said it's simple work. It's not. Not for a single moment. Shame doesn't give up easily. Even after recognizing Shame has to leave, you will still be faced with a drunken text now and then whining for a one-night stay on your couch. Shame will try to guilt you and insist you owe him because, after all, *remember what you did*. But if you let him take one step inside your door, he'll take up the whole couch and will entice you to watch home movies of your darkest moments while stealing any hope of a brighter future. Suddenly and swiftly, Shame can move back in within a flash of entertaining its lies. Y'all. The resolve comes when you daily choose Joy. The final war for cohabitation will be won by consistently shutting the door in Shame's face. Don't relent for one second in your fight for Joy. Either you allow the sum of your darkest memories and mistakes to occupy your thoughts, or you allow Joy to have the remote control and remind you that you are seen, valued, and loved.

You may be reading this and just now became aware that you're even in a fight. Or you may have felt Joy's tug on your life but repeatedly feel stuck or unable or unworthy. Can I be candid? That's Shame sitting on the couch of your heart, enjoying every second of his smug, slobbish behavior. You will not find Joy able to live peacefully with Shame. They are incapable of taking the same space in your thoughts, heart, and decision making.

I'm not usually so blunt or emphatic about a subject unless it's something I believe wholeheartedly to be true. So, this is a moment to pause and hear me if you refuse to hear anything else. You cannot skip this. Don't expect a joyful life while you continually entertain and host lies that seek to steal, kill, and destroy it. Draw up the papers, walk down the hall, and nail the eviction notice to Shame's bedroom door. Kick this spiteful and bullying liar to the curb, throw his belongings out the window, and then change the locks.

Next? Pour yourself a glass of sweet tea, take a deep breath, and put your feet up in your favorite chair because this is the house where Joy lives, and this is where you belong.

Joy
ALWAYS
GIVES
the
benefit
OF
THE
DOUBT.

Chapter 5

SAYING NEVER, MEANING ALWAYS

After our wedding, Chris and I had a normal marriage. And by that I mean we loved each other and life was tough. To understand fully the freedom won by kicking Shame to the curb, I want to be completely honest about the trials we endured until we found a taste of that freedom. I want to lay aside any assumption that embracing freedom is easy. It isn't. And that's where Joy's defiance kicks in and can help us out. Joy isn't just a good time; she's defiant in the worst of times. She is bold and adventurous. Joy leads us to places where we have long refused to venture in our thought life, places that are unhealed and unresolved. Joy pushes against the normal inclinations and patterns we have built in our minds and changes how we speak to ourselves. And, before we know it, we turn a corner to find the most beautiful clearing and spacious freedom for which we've been searching our whole lives.

Have you ever gone for a walk in the thick of the woods and happened upon a small path? The path isn't paved in concrete or even lined with smooth stepping-stones but worn from where others have walked before you. Just well-worn indentations in the dirt that lead through a clearing of dense tree branches that have been slightly pushed back as well.

This is what I imagine our minds look like on the inside when we face Shame daily after the eviction. Shame creates well-worn paths and patterns in our thoughts so that we'll keep coming back to him. These paths are comfortable and safe. They're familiar. And they keep us stuck.

I want you to know, for me, it has taken years to create new paths that direct the way I think about and talk to myself. Even today, I continue to fight to forsake familiar wandering paths that send me back to Shame. I regularly have to clear out new spaces and trail-blaze new walkways in uneven places as I learn to love and forgive myself.

All of that to say, I want you to understand that the joy-filled life is always a journey. I don't want to sneak-attack you with kindness and laughter and leave you feeling as though you were left with empty promises that all will be okay with a pep talk and little effort on your part. It won't. But any new path you must forge to make room for Joy is worth the effort and struggle. I mean, who wouldn't rather endure a season of productive pain than to live a life full of purposeless pain that has no end in sight and keeps you spinning on a wheel like a hamster in a cage? So, pack your backpack with some yummy snacks, grab a bottle of water, and lace up your hiking boots.

I want to take you on a journey that began pushing down the grass and leaves under my feet to discover a new path that eventually saved my marriage.

In spite of all the sexual exchanges I had in relationships before Chris, I was still a virgin on our wedding night. Chris was a virgin, too. Now, listen, I'm not boasting. If it weren't for Chris's resolve, things might have turned out differently. In fact, the night before the wedding, he had gone off to the new apartment we had rented (he was already living there) to prepare a love shanty for our newlywed selves.

Side note: How does one make a love shanty, after all? I imagined Chris lining the hall floor with rose petals, lighting an unnecessary amount of candles throughout the apartment, and playing Barry White music on repeat as he carried me over the threshold.

In reality? He was making the bed, putting down the toilet seat, and making sure the lights were turned off and doors were locked before leaving. There you have it. Love. Shanty. Made.

After our rehearsal dinner, we went to the apartment together. I moved in some more of my belongings, knowing I would no longer live apart from him after the very next day. As we gushed over one another and talked openly about how nervous and excited we were for the wedding, we began to kiss passionately. I found myself saying anything and everything to get him to cave.

I whispered through a kiss upon his neck, "You know, tomorrow night we are gonna be so exhausted . . . we've already done so well waiting; we're practically already married . . . so we don't need to wait tonight."

Nothing. Nada. I swear the man had the resolve of an immovable lid on top of a pickle jar. He smiled slyly and kissed me back and eventually walked me to the door, reassuring me we would have the rest of our lives to make love. Chris was a man on a mission. He knew the only way I could fully understand his love for me was to prove I was worth the wait and deserving of the fight against every natural desire found in a man. He was determined to show me that he loved me for who I was and not for what I could give him. Somehow, Chris knew and loved me so well that this became a "nonnegotiable" in how he would pursue my heart.

Even as I recall this memory, I know how culturally divisive the issue is. I know the currents of love in our society are satisfied in sexual discoveries and explorations sometimes with or without concern for a marital contract. I secretly wish that I could say our resolve to wait for sex until our wedding night was solely a deliberate moral choosing or was tethered to the religious rationale I had grown up hearing. I have to be honest with you. I learned all the rules and still was willing to throw out the rulebook. Chris had not grown up with the same teaching I had, yet *he* was the one developing safe and respectful boundaries. Undoubtedly, the only reason we could both say we were virgins on our wedding night was due to *his* resolve.

The wedding night and honeymoon were . . . well, I will spare details because I am pretty sure my mother and my children will one day long to read this book. I'll say this, y'all. Insert all the winky emojis you can imagine, and then add three more for fun. Each moment was sweeter than the next. And it was FUN!

I remember one night, after building up some much-needed courage to be vulnerable with my new husband, I pulled a special outfit from the secret zippered part of my suitcase. It was my honeymoon, after all, and I had just had a panty party a few weeks earlier. (Some of you may only know them as lingerie showers, but here in the South we call them panty parties.) I was gifted with many sweet and sexy articles of clothing. Some I would have bought for myself . . . some I would have completely passed by.

Then, there's the gift that my sweet mother gave me. I swear she was in denial that her baby girl was about to be married and have a honeymoon. The woman gave me a pair of long-sleeved and long-pant pajamas. Now, to her credit, they were silk and a sexy leopard print. But, y'all. They covered me from neck to ankle. God love her. Bless.

On the other hand, a friend from the church where Chris and I met gave me the most daring gift for my panty party that made me flat-out blush and turn fifty shades of red.

That honeymoon night, I felt it was finally time to try out this little ensemble. I was brave. I was in love. And, with this man of mine, all insecurities left my mind. You'd think putting on less clothing than you normally wear would be easy. Well, you'd be wrong. I marveled at how this tiny piece of clothing could have so many complicated snaps. Slowly my courage about revealing this outfit was fading with wardrobe frustrations. But by this point I had already done the hard work and was not about to let it go to waste.

I opened the bathroom door and went for the most saucy and seductive pose I could imagine. But as I secured my weight on the doorpost, I heard the integrity of those stinking snaps begin to fail me. Before I knew it, I was completely undone. Quite LITERALLY! The force of the snaps caused the front and back flaps to simultaneously fling in opposite directions, violently hitting both sides of my head. Humiliated, I ran back into the bathroom, slammed the door, and yelled, "I need a minute! Don't come in here!" Chris did as most guys would do in that situation. He laughed and laughed. And *then* he realized he needed to calm me down and comfort my embarrassment. Oh man, y'all. We have some of the craziest memories. One reason I share that with you today is because it shows how being in love and being loved for who you are inspires you to try things you'd never have tried before. When you feel freedom for the first time, you take risks. When things don't go as planned, you either can laugh it up or hide away, promising to never try again. I'll spare you the details, but I sure didn't hide away for too long.

Now, sad to say, (like most every newlywed couple) the honeymoon eventually ended.

We moved into our sweet 720-square-foot apartment.

We laughed a lot.

We watched movies late at night and made chocolate chip cookies at two o'clock in the morning.

We slept in late when we could, and began our forever-best-friend sleepover.

Isn't that what we all like to think marriage is going be? Forever fun? But, guess what? Somewhere along the way, you have your first disagreement. You have arguments about money or how you grew up doing things one way and want your spouse to bend to your liking. The dishes stay in the sink a night too many and you have a stand-off as to who is going to do them. You slowly discover that your forever-best-friend sleepover isn't as much fun when you add in all the responsibilities of being an adult as well.

What I have since discovered about marriage between a man and woman is this: Testosterone and estrogen were not meant to live peacefully together without compromise and unconditional love. Y'all. Marriage is flipping hard. If I'm completely honest, I was still struggling under fictions swirling in my mind that I wasn't worth being loved. Shame kept calling me back down the well-worn paths. And Chris was in a fight of his own that I think many men can identify with: learning how to overcome and manage anger better than his father had before him. Now, I've heard it said that vulnerability leads to deeper intimacy. Well, if that is true, it's also true that my insecurities began to surface the more intimate we became emotionally and physically. I willingly grew less vulnerable as I followed familiar paths of fear and shame. I'd find myself picking up breadcrumbs on trails that spoke to me the well-known voice of condemnation and unworthiness. Then, one night, in one careless conversation,

I foolishly thought I had all the justification I needed to derail any efforts I'd previously made to let Chris into my heart.

That particular night we had opened up about new things we would like to try (like all good newlyweds do after dinner). We were being vulnerable with each other because we had built our relationship on trust.

And then, without warning, as if it were a reckless blow to a piñata from a toddler at his birthday party, Chris told me something I was hoping never to hear. And in that moment, the realization shocked me like ice-cold water that we had very different expectations about intimacy. He opened up, and I shut down.

And wouldn't you know it? The customary musings of shame flooded over me with a million "I-told-you-sos." While Chris never intended this, his words drummed up all my old familiar feelings of unworthiness. And I began to think that for all the ways I had so negligently given myself to other men, I now deserved this in my marriage as a *punishment*.

To say we had entered a season of sexual struggles was a vast understatement. We were quickly and inescapably growing more distant both physically and emotionally. I felt overwhelmed with this idea that my portion in life was an unhappy and unsatisfied marriage. Even worse, I deserved my portion and, by golly, there were starving children in other countries and I'd better clean my plate of frustration and discontent . . . even if I had to force-feed myself the failures. Over the next couple of years, disconnect became the norm despite the sporadic sexual obligations we fulfilled in our role as "husband and wife," and there grew a new monster that would seek to destroy my joy: body shame . . . to the "nth" degree.

Until that moment, it was easy to ignore the true feelings I felt about my body, thanks to laughter, jokes, and tacos. On average, I didn't find myself consumed with thoughts about how I looked. I would just gaze into the mirror and think, *Get it, girl. Pretty eyes and chunky thighs. Now, kill 'em dead.* However, body shame tangled with my newly presumed punishment. I am not speaking about wanting to change small things about my physical appearance. No, this was a deeper attachment to a thought that my body wasn't meant to be enjoyed, admired, or appreciated. And, wrapped within that was the natural assumption that I was to deny enjoyment, admiration, and appreciation for my body as well. This distortion spilled over into every area of my life. It hit our marriage like a professional NFL defensive lineman as I pulled away emotionally from the man who meant every single promise he had ever made and would spend his life doing everything possible to make them a reality.

It also migrated over into the internal conversations I would have with myself on a daily basis. Slowly and subtly at first, Shame came knocking at my door again. And against my better judgment, I let him start replaying all those old tapes about how I wasn't enough, wasn't worth it, wasn't *really* known or loved after all. Most obviously, it affected the massive amount of weight I would allow this unappreciated body to carry. I'd feed my disappointments with enormous amounts of food and began an addiction to sweets and anything fried that would ultimately top me off at 360 pounds. Truth be told, I could have weighed more . . . I'll never know because our scales at home maxed out at that number when I stood on them.

I had reached the lowest of lows, and Chris was beside himself as he saw the spark and fire flicker inside me. I know we had vowed to love each other *all* our days, whether good or bad, but in my naïvety I believed those days would solely be determined by external circumstances. I couldn't even fathom that the bad days would be fixed by internal struggles and regrets. Like many new couples, I thought it would be "you and me, baby, against the world," which is kind of sexy, really. Ironically, I believe I was more prepared to combat sickness or poverty or infertility with this man when I promised "in good and bad, in sickness or in health, for richer, for poorer." There was no doomsday prep for the havoc body shame and regret would have upon my marriage as I shared the ever-hopeful kiss on that December wedding altar. I didn't realize that some of the biggest battles we would face together would happen inside our hearts. And I wasn't alone in responding poorly.

Chris preferred anger. He was never fully angry at me, nor was he angry at me for being overweight. Shoot, the man married a very full-figured woman. No, Chris was angry because he felt disconnected from the cold shell I had become. Where was the spitfire he promised the rest of his days to have and to hold? I honestly believe that anger is a response to a fear or feeling of helplessness or hopelessness. I know his battle was never against me. No, his response was to act out as his father had shown him in moments of being pressed, crushed, disappointed, and powerless.

Chris struggled against his natural inclination to be a lover and force-fed himself a new role in our marriage: fighter. He acted out in fiery explosions of hurtful words that would, in turn, affirm my doubts. He would resort to cussing me out to win every argument. I know now that Chris hated the way I was treating myself and putting myself down, so he reacted the best way he knew at the time: like a drill sergeant would inspire a fresh troop of recruits, yelling and ordering me to "get my crap together." But how could I do that? How could I just break free from shame and learn to love myself wholly? I lacked passion in every area of my life. I was trying to escape who I was and what I felt I deserved, in any way imaginable. I wasn't experiencing a life filled with joy . . . not in any respect.

The struggles that Chris and I experienced aren't uncommon and, unfortunately, may be tame compared to the strains you've experienced in your past or current relationships. I never want to magnify my struggles compared with yours. I only offer my experiences and the journey I have traveled to embrace freedom and live with defiant joy. Your journey may look vastly different at the end of your days. However, we all share some commonalities along the path.

One is the ability to choose how to respond to disappointments, our regrets, the toughness of life. No matter how helpless you feel in your circumstances, circumstances ain't got nothing on joy. No matter what you're facing, you can choose joy any time, at any moment you please. And it might just make all the difference.

It's amazing how fast we can jump in our mind to an unfavorable outcome. In the thick of disappointment, we are hasty to allow our imaginations to run wild and never offer ourselves or others the benefit of the doubt.

Joy isn't like that. Joy is born from hope—hoping for the best in people and then believing in them enough to give them the benefit of the doubt. Hope is vital to joy's survival. To truly have joy in our relationships, we must trail-blaze new paths that lead us out of shame and into new possibilities.

I get it. It seems easier to throw in the towel and just walk away from the fight for Joy in your relationships when you've been disappointed. Nevertheless, Joy rests inside the clutches of Hope. And, if I am completely honest, this is my favorite thing about my dear friend Joy. She rarely wastes a single moment walking down a path of remorse. Joy looks toward the days ahead in gleeful expectation of the best. Hope fuels her every step forward as she believes the best about those she loves and looks forward to every new adventure just around the bend. It's not that she looks at the world and its circumstances with rose-tinted lenses or lives in denial or naïvety. She knows that everyone can be afforded a bad day or two. Joy gives the benefit of the doubt when the "ugly" unexpectedly shows up. Without the constant welcome and warm friendship of Joy, it is counterintuitive to trust and hope when we find ourselves faced with hurts, mistakes, and failures from those we have allowed in our inner circle. But counterintuitive is all part of Joy's charm—she surprises us all the time.

Isn't it just like most of us to give up quickly when our expectations don't mirror the realities in our relationships? And I'm not just speaking of romantic relationships. Whether the friction is caused by the authorities that govern us, the family member with whom we have a long-standing grudge, the cashier who doesn't validate our coupon, or the people who live in the same space with us daily, our primary impulse is to give up on others.

The great author and poet Maya Angelou once stated, "When someone shows you who they are, believe them the first time."

If they show you they are good-hearted though imperfect people just trying to do their best, believe them.

If they show you they are only in this rodeo for themselves and don't care what expense that bears on others, you can believe that too.

Our actions say a lot about who we are.

But remember, we all have days when we mess up and do it wrong. Per our human nature, we too quickly assume the worst in others at the very first pass. We are more comfortable (note, I did *not* say comforted, but comfortable) with assigning blame and pushing others away at first error.

For some strange reason, we have become a people who demand perfection from every other human being with whom we relate. From the demands for perfection hidden in our minds for our dream spouse, the perfect child, or the ideal boss, it's as if we forget we're imperfect people ourselves. As I've stated before, we're all amateurs at life, figuring out how to love others and, even more importantly, how to love ourselves. I knew if I were to have authentic joy daily in my home and marriage, I needed to have some grace with Chris, and most importantly, myself. I needed to see beyond a single moment of disappointment and hope for better days ahead. I needed to be vulnerable and forgiving. I needed to be honest.

If there's anything that can suck Joy from your days, it's resigning in haste from relationships that might be salvaged otherwise. I fully believe the adage, "No man or woman is an island." We crave relationship because we were created for relationship. If you think about what is most important to you, I am confident it's attached to a person in some way, shape, or form. Family. Friendship. Marriage. Love. Romance. Joy is in each one of these relationships, because there is no greater joy in life than being known and loved. And, if she is going to not only survive, but thrive, she must be liberated to give hope to these relationships so that they can be authentic in their successes and losses. Joy gives permission to fail and offers forgiveness instead of a cold shoulder.

I know this to be true because I have stood at the crossroads of staying in the fight or abandoning my post in my marriage. Joy is a choice, and it is a choice that will be tested.

I will never forget a fight that Chris and I had while our daughter was young and I was seven months pregnant with our son. Though I've tried to recall how it even started, I cannot nor can Chris. Believe me. I have asked.

All I remember is that it was in front of our daughter, Cadence. She was only twelve months old; I was feeding her baby food from a jar as fiery explosions of accusations and hurtful screams were hurled back and forth. If you've never experienced a full-on verbal assault with a baby in the same room, you may never understand how devastating this was to a momma's heart. As weaponized words and profanity flew between us, I watched Cadence's little body begin to hold all our hurt and hate. She pouted out her tiny lip and started to cry an inconsolable cry. I scooped her up and tried to comfort her tears, but it was too late. With her small frame resting on my folded arm, I patted her gently on the back and rocked side to side pacing the kitchen floor, still cussing out Chris as I did. Y'all. I tense up even now as I recall this memory. It is one of my deepest regrets both in parenting and in our marriage.

Eventually, Chris shut down the argument by abandoning it altogether and slamming the door behind him. As he drove away from the heated conflict just as he had done before in almost every fight of this magnitude, I felt with terror and certainty that the only recourse was to walk out of my marriage. I knew he would come back after he cooled off. But this time I didn't want to be there when he did. I just didn't know how we could go on like this.

I spent the following hour calming Cadence, putting her to sleep in her car seat, and packing my bags with things I would need to live for a week or so. I called my sister in tears and asked if I could stay with her. I told her I was going to leave my husband—and I meant it. There was a resolve in me to bail on everything we had built together in the years prior. I was miserable and full of discontent with Chris. I feared the future. I was void of all hope for my marriage. Y'all. By now, I was most certainly miles down the trail of my all-too-familiar path of shame, fear, and despair.

My sister was more than willing to accommodate her very pregnant sister and niece. However, she also reminded me that I had married a good man and that everyone was afforded a bad day. She asked me to imagine what it may look like if I stayed and tried just one more day. Whether she knew it or not, she was the light on my darkened trail showing me a new path toward hope and joy. Joy imagines with empathy and compassion what the next second, minute, or hour could hold if you chose to forgive and hope. My sister was the voice of Joy crying out to me, giving me courage to take some difficult steps into the unknown thicket before me. Before I hung up the phone, I took her advice to heart and promised to stay one more night. I may have seen it possible to change my path, but I was still very hurt and angry. Despite my promise to stay one more night, I had every intention to head to her home the very next day.

Late the same evening, Chris walked back in the door, per his usual behavior after these heated fights. Refusing to make eye contact, he walked past me toward our bedroom. That night we slept as strangers sharing a park bench for a bed on the street corner. Back to back, nearly two feet separating us, I cried myself to sleep. I grieved this man I had loved and who was now more distant than I ever envisioned possible. I grieved the marriage I once dreamed about as a child that I now saw as a fleeting vision. I grieved the idea of co-parenting with Chris. I saw how loving and gentle he was with Cadence and the way his eyes lit up when we saw the first sonogram revealing I was pregnant with our son. Chris was a good daddy. I grieved the thought of my children dividing time, homes, possessions, and holidays between us. I was heartbroken.

By the time morning came, I had cried more in one night than I had in years. My tears had become my pillow. I knew it was possible to leave Chris and live life on my own. I knew I could be strong enough to do it if I needed to. I knew I would make any and every sacrifice that it would take to raise our children alone. Nevertheless, I didn't want to do that. All those tears brought clarity when I realized the very reason I was grieving was because I didn't *want* out of my marriage. I wanted Chris. I wanted all the things I spent the night hours lamenting. What's more, I wanted to feel beautiful and passionate again. I wanted to be free from shame and the physical weight mounted upon my bones. I wanted the fire in my eyes to return. I knew I needed Hope if I was ever to find Joy again. I had lost all sight of her. And, if I was ever going to see her again, I needed to muster up optimism that this was, indeed, our worst day, but it wouldn't be our last day.

I hope you'll hear me on this. Bookmark this page and promise me you'll come back to it when the going gets tough. Because this is a promise you can stand on:

YOU MAY BE LIVING YOUR WORST DAY.

BUT, GRAB ON TO HOPE THAT IT ISN'T YOUR LAST DAY.

I needed to believe that the days ahead of us were brighter than the darkness we were living. I needed to start imagining again—that I had hope for change, that Chris had hope for change, that we could be better together. That we weren't bound to keep walking the well-worn paths that had gotten us into this mess in the first place.

I chose to hold on for dear life to the words that my sister had said; I decided to give Chris the benefit of the doubt. It seemed he had done some soul-searching that night as well. As Chris left for work, he kissed our daughter atop her forehead as I fed her a bottle in my lap. He looked at me and said, "I love you. We'll talk if you want when I get home from work." During Cadence's naptime, I spent the next two hours praying over my marriage.

I had a moment of clarity when I realized I wanted to make a list of all the things I would *never* do in my marriage in order to make it work. Such things as:

- ✦ I will never leave.
- ✦ I will never hold a grudge.

- I will never assume the worst of Chris.
- I will never keep a record of wrongs.
- I will never be quick to condemn our relationship.

And the list went on. I read and reread the list aloud. Something didn't sit right as I read it. I kept on hearing the phrase my mom would say while I was growing up: "Never say never." I then listened to an inner voice challenge me to change every *never* to an *always*. I began to cross out the previous list which I naïvely thought had so much wisdom. I saw the marked-out phrases and wondered how to replace them. So, I began to change my thinking altogether. This was the moment when I didn't just hear the call to get off the beaten path where Shame always led me astray. No, this was the moment I lifted my foot and took the first step to turn around, change my thoughts about my marriage, and embrace the freedom of the new adventure surely to follow.

Scared and exhilarated, I began to make a new list:

- I will always stay.
- I will always forgive.
- I will always hope for the best in Chris.
- I will always wipe the slate clean at the end of the day.
- I will always champion and fight for our marriage.

I don't know what came over me next, other than to describe it as a peace that withstood my circumstances. For the first time, joy seemed possible in my home and marriage again. Quite the opposite of what had been a visceral reaction to stay hopeful, I was making a deliberate choice to do something, not just evade something. My list of "nevers" was holding me under a regime of obligation and reaction. My list of "always" was freeing me to stay positive toward my circumstances while developing characteristics of the person I always wanted to display. My "always" declarations were freeing me to feel again. And they reminded me that joy is a choice—that even in the face of uncontrollable circumstances, I always have control over how I choose to respond.

Joy reminded me that if I was going to keep my marriage alive and to live an abundant, forward-moving life, I had to shift from saying *never* and begin meaning *always*.

Here's the dirty truth about Shame: it's reactive. It's passive. Something happens to bring us shame, and we allow that emotion to take control of our lives. Shame convinces us to believe that we *don't have a choice* at all. Shame says, "That's it; you're doomed; you're done. There's nothing you can do to change your fate." Joy, on the other hand, is active. Joy doesn't let circumstances call the shots—she activates her free will to decide how she will respond to anything life swings her way. She's empowering! Because she takes back control from Shame and says "no more," I get to decide how this challenge will shape me and how I will respond to it.

I sat at our kitchen table and stared for a long time at the flame of a decorative candle I had lit earlier. Suddenly, I had an idea. At that moment, I didn't even know how to begin to tackle a single issue of body shame. But I did know

I had a choice to make about my marriage. I wrote the word *DIVORCE* on a piece of paper in big, black permanent marker, set it inside the candle flame, and watched it burn. I felt empowered to hope once again as I gazed at the paper word being reduced to ash. My decision had been made. I was choosing *always*.

Chris came home early from work, and we both apologized, forgave each other, and reset the atmosphere in our home. But this time, we didn't hedge our bets that we would react better during our next argument. No, we began making an offensive plan.

The first practical thing we promised to "always" do was so simple. We promised we would always love and hope for the best in each other. I don't know if you've ever experienced a toxic cycle of bringing up past failures to try to win arguments, but we had a horrible habit of revisiting our past in each and every fight. We changed all of that that day. We made new promises that if we were going to fight, we would always fight to see the best in one another. We promised we would leave the past behind us as lessons learned, not as inescapable character assignments. And we would look to the future instead. It wasn't easy or an immediate fix, but we definitively began to make strides to keep our marriage alive and awesome. We committed to the journey, come what may, together.

Let me tell you, it's a wonderful thing to make vows to each other on one of the best days of your life—your wedding day. But it's a whole new level to make those vows to each other once again after one of the *worst* days of your life together. And that kind of strength and resolve you can trust.

To this day, we often reset and remind each other, without a doubt, that divorce isn't an option for us. We've taken it off the table completely. Even more so, our "yes" is always on the table. Meaning, we will always do whatever it takes to offer each other the best we are, not just prep for how to react when faced with the worst we are. To experience a joy that gives the benefit of the doubt, we had to move from saying "never" to meaning "always."

Joy offers hope when it seems hopeless. As you read this, you may be at the end of your rope. You may feel stuck in a fog with no hope in sight. I don't assume to understand your personal journey or a path I haven't traveled. But, friend . . . I do know what being on the wrong path feels like. I know what it's like to feel stuck in the same ruts over and over again, to feel like you're doomed to repeat history. But Hope gives us a way to trail-blaze a new path and a fresh start. When we believe that, the future can be bright again. I love what this passage from the Bible says in a modern translation:

> Summing it all up, friends, I'd say you'll do best by filling your minds and meditating on things true, noble, reputable, authentic, compelling, gracious—the best, not the worst; the beautiful, not the ugly; things to praise, not things to curse.
>
> *Philippians 4:8 (The Message)*

Plant your feet firmly on the unknown adventures wherever they lead you, as you hold out hope for the best within yourself and those closest to you. I *know* what it feels like to have hope resurrect and usher in a new breath of life-bringing joy to the caverns of a resentful heart. I don't know the specifics of your unwritten lists, but can I encourage you in this way? Quit the defensive game and go on the offense. Press on toward a goal to win whatever you're dealt in this life. Go ahead. List your "nevers" plainly, but plan your "always'" purposefully.

Because when you exchange the familiar paths of Shame to blaze new trails toward Joy, the terrain might be rougher and it might be unknown, but you will always be trading up.

Joy
DOESN'T FEAR
"WHAT IFS" BUT
HOPES for
WHAT can BE.

Chapter 6

FROM WHAT IF TO WHY NOT

Long before becoming Chewbacca Mom, I became a momma in real life. Surprisingly, I was honestly content if we never had children. I know a lot of women may say this but never truly mean it. But I did. I fully proposed it for seven years of our marriage. Whenever I would hear the tick-tock of my biological clock begin to tick, we'd entertain the conversation about having children and instead get another plant or animal to practice keeping alive and healthy. Chris and I knew we needed to overcome a mound of struggles before intentionally trying to add tiny humans that would likely perpetuate our behaviors.

But a church mission trip to an orphanage in Zambia changed all that. No matter the issues Chris and I had those first seven years of our marriage, I began to see the sincere need for someone to rescue, love, and protect these beautiful children—abandoned or lost—with the love only a good mother and father could offer them. And, reduced to even more truth, I knew I needed to grow up. (Listen. I'm not one for abandoning play and childlike wonder. However, I knew there was a world of hurt around me in which I could make a difference. Growing up meant abandoning selfishness and embracing a heart that sees and loves others in need. Shoot. I'd best keep my childlike joy at every opportunity, I guess!)

I knew that Chris and I were in a pattern of repetitive behavior that certainly needed to end. And so, a fierce desire was suddenly born in me to have a family of our own.

Have you ever prayed for something so intensely that you lost time amidst your tears and requests to God? On the last night of the mission trip, I wept and prayed for most of the dark hours, begging God to allow the desire for me to be a momma to become a reality, saying my "Amen" only as the sun began to rise. I knew it best to not leave all those prayers floating in the African air as I packed for my flight home the next day. I had encountered this profound shift in my ambitions fully apart from my husband and now had to travel several hours rehearsing the perfect way to explain to him my newfound desire to start a family.

I made it through customs without a hiccup, hiked down to baggage claim, and nervously approached my guy who was waiting for me. Y'all. I couldn't have been more excited to see him and hold him. He could sense something was different in our embrace. He could feel in my hug an internal change that had scratched the surface, returning a tiny bit of passion for life to his bride. Chris pulled away, smiled the classic sly half-smile I know so well, kissed me on the forehead, grabbed my luggage, and walked me to our car. He knew I had just spent weeks in Africa and made sure to drive us to the nearest taco joint to show me love the greatest way he knew how. Yes. Glorious tacos, y'all. (The sixth love language is tacos, if no one has officially told you this before. The seventh love language is sleep. Most females know this. Let a woman sleep in and feed her tacos; you will win her love and affection.)

I waited until we were full of crispy shells and pico de gallo, worked up my courage, and finally confessed my desire to be a momma. I acknowledged how we had danced around this issue for years as well as the fact that we weren't fully healed in every aspect of our marriage. I also knew without a doubt that it was time to start the conversation and stop looking at pug puppy adoption websites to fill a very real void for a baby. (Although there's something precious about a furbaby, I had a deep longing and invitation to motherhood I had never heard before.)

I asked Chris to allow me to verbally process every thought without interruption, because I was fearful I would gloss over details or recant my intentions based on his reaction. I couldn't and wouldn't give doubt a stage. I knew I was meant to be a momma, just as I knew I was meant to be his wife. I knew in my heart it was time for us to try for a family. My last words assured him that I didn't need a hasty response and that I wouldn't bring it up again until he spoke about it first. And, with very little reaction, he promised he'd be the next to bring it up.

A few days passed as Chris and I returned to our familiar rhythms and routines. I honestly wasn't stressed or pressured to try to make something happen for us to become pregnant. I was calm and confident of the promises that I believed I heard in the stillness of my soul about becoming a momma.

Ironically, my birthday fell on Mother's Day that year, and that was the day Chris brought up the topic again. I was desperately hoping this was going to be a favorable conversation. I sure didn't want to be depressed on my birthday/Mother's Day by him squashing the idea of starting a family.

In the morning hours before we left for the busyness of our day, Chris wanted to take a private moment to give me a present. Inside a gift bag filled with tissue paper was a cardboard box and inside the box was a Willow Tree® figurine of a pregnant woman. If you could have seen the confusion on my face, I'm pretty sure you would have chuckled. *Was my husband making fun of me in gift form?* I wondered. Cruel, y'all. Just downright dirty.

Chris quickly saw the confusion and spoke up. He revealed he had felt the same shift in his desires to be a daddy the very same night I was across the ocean pouring out my heart to God. Chris found the figurine while I was still in Africa, bought it, wrapped it, and kept it as a surprise for my upcoming birthday. He intentionally bought it as a "faith-for-the-future" gift for Mother's Day as a way of declaring his hopeful desires that the next year we would either be with child or well on our journey to adopt.

He done good, y'all. Chris had never looked more attractive to me than at that moment. I do believe I actually said, "Awwwwwwwwwwwwwwwww," out loud for more than five minutes. Naturally, part two of my birthday gift came that night—a night we shall not soon forget, if you follow me. And five weeks later, we discovered we were pregnant.

Imagine, however, if you can, a pre-Pinterest world. I didn't have a very creative way to unbox gender color-reveal balloons or announce in some never-before-seen creative way that he was gonna become a daddy.

Instead, I got a pregnancy test from the local dollar store, went into the tiny hall bathroom of our double-wide trailer, took it out of the package, and peed in a cup. As I waited for the test to reveal the results, my stomach felt as though I had dropped from the highest point of the Tower of Terror at Disney World. A pink line appeared. Slowly, a second pink line began to reveal itself. However, it wasn't very bold. It was a shy, little pink line. So shy that I remember calling out to Chris, "Hey, hon, can you come help me with something?" I'm pretty sure that's not what every guy wants to hear from his wife while she's in the bathroom. Nevertheless, he reluctantly shuffled down the hall and peeked in the door.

I handed the test to him and said, "Hey. So. What does this look like to you?" Chris's eyes bounced back and forth as he read the instructions on the open box and looked at the two pink lines on the pregnancy test. He gulped a giant gulp and replied, "Uh. I don't know. Are you pregnant?"

To say that I failed at making a moment of the news is an understatement. We were just two crazy-excited, slightly-terrified parents-to-be huddled in a bathroom over a pee stick, joining the throngs of many who had gone before us.

To make amends, after the first sonogram, I brought home pictures of our baby, then resembling a Frito corn chip, framed with a bag of Fritos next to it on our kitchen counter. Genius. As a matter of fact, we spent the next few months calling this unborn child "Frito" before we found out that we were, indeed, having a baby girl.

Chris and I spent the following weeks dreaming and planning. The newfound happiness in our home was wonderful. I found myself humming as I walked from room to room in our dilapidated trailer. Suddenly, I didn't mind household chores. I was excited to tell everyone the news. I had a skip in my step, and surely my face must have beamed with the "pregnant woman's glow."

I even wrote a couple of notes and poems to this unknown and unseen, yet certainly hoped for and prayed for, child. For kicks and grins, I pulled out the old notes and writings just for you. And here you thought this book wouldn't have any poetry. Well, be prepared to be amazed, or at the very minimum, amused. I present from the annals of Facebook in the category of "notes" from my personal page:

WHIRLWIND . . .

August 18, 2008, at 11:40 a.m.

God is so funny and faithful all at the same time. I forget that He doesn't operate in the confines of time. So many times . . . do I forget.

I have complained about wanting to accomplish so many things before I turn 30.

How pathetic am I?

Really. I must apologize for the whining drama.

So, since the complaints and grumbles, God has shown up in a whirlwind.

I can't help but think of Abraham and the promise God gave him about having a child and being the father of many nations and how he would possess a land that was under his very feet, yet he still found himself fatherless, fearful, and homeless . . . for a long while. God didn't forget His promise. He has an appointed time for everything and is not confined to time in any way. So, yeah . . . that is so relevant to the whirlwind in which God has shown His promises to me.

Yesterday, I became 14 weeks pregnant. What?! There are many women that have been mothers before and will continue to be . . . however; I am overwhelmed at this idea of being a mother . . . a mom . . . I still feel like a kid in so many ways. And now we have a new home? What in the world has happened? Chris and I just started feeling like there was a time to start trying for all this in May. It's now three months later, three months pregnant, and two nights in a bed in a new home . . . and six months until another person lives with us. And my emotions in all of this?

I am more in love with Chris than ever before . . . he is my rock, my best friend, my one true love that shows me love unconditionally. He honors me and cares for me.

I am scared for the responsibility of raising a child . . . hoping that it won't be in counseling over the way I treated him/her when it's in its 30s.

I am nesting . . . enough said. HGTV is my drug of choice. Back off!

I am missing my childhood and all the while relishing the joys yet to come as I step into the deep end of the pool.

Seriously. A whirlwind. God is faithful. God is always good.

Well, that one was fun. It seems as though we somehow knew our then-living-situation was more a money pit than purchasing a home would be. Upon finding we were pregnant, we started looking for a home that would be more family friendly.

Let's look at another one, shall we? Once again, thank you, Facebook annals. Nothing like a little #ThrowbackThursday or Time Hop to take us back. This note was written only ten days following as I began to think on what it would be like to hold my child for the first time. I gushed as thoughts swirled in my head about this intense change of becoming a mom.

FOR WHAT'S INSIDE

August 28, 2008, at 12:03 p.m.

I love you so much . . . and I've never seen your face.

I'm closer to you and you closer to me than I've ever experienced . . . and I've never even touched your skin.

Throughout the day, I feel the effects of you with flutters in my very soul.

Throughout the night, I sleep gently with you as you hear the calm of my resting heart.

You

are

remarkable!

I've haven't wanted to meet someone for the first time the way that I long to meet you.

Do you think I'll cry with joy when I see you the first time?

I do . . .

I will love you more today than yesterday.

However, that still won't be as much as I love you tomorrow.

There's a good thing about the love I can offer you . . .

It's not my own. Mine couldn't ever be enough.

How I can't wait to care for you!

to comfort you.

to hear your cries.

to see your joys.

I await this life with you . . . to know you more.

You are so REMARKABLE to me!

How precious is a new momma's heart, right? I remember feeling all those emotions as they swept over me. But why would I share this mushy, gushy, overly embarrassing stuff? Because these romanticized hopes and dreams for the future were followed by what became the most difficult two years of my life. I cling to these romanticized moments because they are the only silver lining to the storm cloud that could have taken my life and killed my marriage. While the beginnings of my pregnancy were wonder-filled, the ending was considerably different. Not only that, but my second pregnancy was worse than I could ever have imagined.

Near the middle of my first pregnancy, I discovered I had gestational diabetes. According to a 2014 analysis by the Centers for Disease Control and Prevention, the prevalence of gestational diabetes is as high as 9.2 percent. It starts when your body is not able to make and use all the insulin it needs for pregnancy. This is not good for your body, but it's even worse for the baby, and can lead to the little one being born prematurely with undeveloped lungs and organs, or to a more tragic outcome: stillbirth.

I was promptly classified as a high-risk pregnancy and began to see a specialist and dietician once a week. I would self-check insulin levels throughout the day with pricks for blood samples from my fingers and thighs. Daydreaming about the perfect baby delivery story was replaced with four self-administered daily injections of insulin to my stomach. We had a new mortgage, a baby on the way, and a heap of medical bills and expenses accruing each and every day.

Despite the gloomy odds ahead of us, I kept my eyes on the prize of being a momma. There wasn't a thing that I wouldn't do to see my daughter and hold her safely in my arms. I followed doctor's orders, kept a food journal, and made all my appointments on time. Finally, the day came, and I felt a peace that all was going to be well. Labor lasted twelve hours before needing to call in my OBGYN to make the formal introductions between my Cadee-bug and me.

When I first held my daughter, I wanted it to be like all the scenes I had watched in the movies. I just knew I was going to be a blubbering hot mess of tears and varied emotions. But that wasn't the scenario at all. I held her, made sure she had all ten fingers and toes, then looked in her eyes, smiled, and said to her, "Hi, sweet girl! I'm your momma. I'm so glad to meet you!" Then the nurses swept her from my arms to begin cleaning her and weighing her as they normally do.

Next, I began negotiations with Chris to find me a taco or a cheeseburger as soon as humanly possible. I was rejoicing that I was no longer pregnant and could eat something fatty again. Hashtag "glory." That's right. Hashtag that word in your mind. Because the first taste of that cheeseburger was glorious.

My daughter was born in January, on an unusually cold and icy Texas day. Chris found a moment to brave the conditions to go home and bring back some creature comforts missing from the hospital room. I may or may not have had him bring a bottle of air freshener and some jarred candles that smell amazing when lit. While he was gone, Cadence was asleep in my arms, content after a feeding. As I studied her face, I was overwhelmed with affection for her. I knew there wasn't a day that I wouldn't spend loving her in all my life. I knew what it meant for the first time to love someone with no conditions. As she slept, I sang to her the Disney song that Dumbo's mom sang to him, "Baby Mine." (You know by now how I love my Disney.) All felt right and safe and peaceful.

The gestational diabetes was leaving my body as my hormones began to regulate back to normal. However, something else crept in to take its place.

I had heard of the phrase "the baby blues" at various times in my life. The weeks following giving birth to Cadence, I would know full well what that phrase meant.

I woke up one morning, looked at Chris, and felt absolutely nothing for him. I knew his love for Cadence was strong. I knew that he loved me as well. But what my mind knew became completely disconnected from how I felt, and that's when things got confusing. For reasons I cannot explain, I did not know why I had married him, how I fell in love with him, nor how I was going to spend the rest of my life with him.

Chris could tell I was beginning to distance myself from him. He could sense it every morning he would go to hug me or grab my hips as he stood behind me, and every night when we went to sleep and I stayed far away from him in bed. Empty of emotion, I finally told him that I didn't know if I loved him any longer or could ever love him again. I wish there were a particular grudge or rational reason that made me feel that way. But there wasn't. I just know I didn't know why I had fallen in love with him to begin with, nor how to fake feeling fine being with him daily now. Tired of pretending, I told him all the dark thoughts I was having toward him.

Chris calmly said to me the wisest and most reassuring words: "Well. You'd better figure it out because I'm not going anywhere." He both calmed me and annoyed me with his resolve to stay and fight for us. And, although he'd never say it, I knew he understood there was more to my disconnect than just intense emotions.

I was more than sleep deprived and exhausted. A whole tangled mess of chemicals and hormones was at work in my brain and body, and it was crazy-making. My thoughts disturbed me and did not feel like my own. This daily life of motherhood I had dreamed about for so long was warping into a nightmare. I slowly began realizing I was facing the same battle with depression I had faced in college. I was, in fact, enduring full-blown postpartum depression and needed an intervention.

In spite of my efforts to push Chris away emotionally and physically, the man never gave up on me. He came home from work one night to surprise me with a "family date." We prepared a million items needed to take a newborn out into public, hopped in the car, and he drove us to our favorite Mexican food restaurant. And, for the first time in about eight weeks, we had a meal uninterrupted by a diaper change or bottle feeding. As we talked, something remarkable happened. I looked across the table and saw my husband. I didn't just look at him. No, I saw him. I saw the effort he was making to love me when I was deliberately pushing him away. I saw every ounce of everything wonderful that made me fall in love with him in the beginning. It was as though the light shining down from our tabletop chandelier was glowing brighter and brighter over his head.

I felt immediate remorse for the way I had been treating him, and finally safe and loved enough to confess every dark, destructive thought I was keeping locked internally in shame. I reached out and made him grab my hands and apologized for being so cold. I told him I needed help. It was as if I could finally see through the dense fog that had been clouding my better judgment.

Following that date night, I made an appointment to seek treatment once again to level out my hormone levels and fight depression with medication. I finished a couple of months of pills and slowly, day by day, I returned to myself. As the fog cleared, the colors of life returned.

Chris and I started to reconnect in every way in our marriage. I mean, as much as possible with a newborn in the same house. And trust me, after learning the hard way how the baby blues affected me, we took extra birth control precautions. Three forms of birth control, to be exact.

Despite our efforts, I sensed I might need to take a pregnancy test just a few short weeks later. So, off to the dollar store I went. While Chris was at work and Cadence was taking a nap, I took the test and discovered I was indeed pregnant again. I would love to say that I was overjoyed. And well, I was sure over-something. I was scared to death. I had just started to feel normal, and now I was about to face once more every obstacle I had just overcome.

I didn't believe I was strong enough. I was confused, frustrated, and angry. Chris got home from work and walked into the kitchen where I was feeding Cadence. If I had failed miserably at announcing the first time I got pregnant, this time would be even worse. I looked at him and said as bluntly as possible, "I need to tell you something." Chris must have seen the fear in my eyes because he backed up against the counter, hopped up, and sat with feet dangling and the biggest, widest eyes of expectation I had ever seen on his face.

"I'm pregnant. Again." The words dropped and shattered like a prized antique family heirloom breaking against the cold ceramic tile. Chris jumped down, held me close, and reassured me that this was good news and not bad news. He had a vision of the future I couldn't see. And, if I were completely honest, I rode the coattails of his optimism and hope for the next nine months.

I scheduled another appointment and exam with my doctor only to discover that I had developed gestational diabetes much more swiftly than my first pregnancy and needed to see a specialist again. Later, I walked into the specialist's office with all the hope I could muster up that we would make the most of this pregnancy and he would have the map I needed to make it out with both my health and this child's health intact.

Only this hopeful journey wasn't the conversation he offered. In fact, he didn't waste any time bringing up the idea that Chris and I may want to terminate the pregnancy altogether because my hormones and body hadn't had the time it needed to recoup after my first pregnancy. I remember him shaking his head with a downward nod and an unspoken "tsk, tsk." To say the specialist lacked a good bedside manner is a grave understatement. He quickly prescribed the all-too-familiar insulin routine and demanded I see him and my dietician once a week.

Each time we would meet, he would tell me how dire the pregnancy was, mentioning the what-ifs and possible adverse outcomes. He spent cumulative hours telling me the necessary steps we'd need to explore if my child was born too prematurely or stillborn. This doctor offered little hope that both my unborn child and I would make it through this pregnancy alive and well.

I responded to the negative outlook with a huge disconnect. Even discovering the most incredible news that we were having a boy, each day I grew more pregnant, I shut down any expectancy of ever seeing a happy and healthy son born to me. I wasn't writing fancy-schmancy poems about meeting *this* baby. Y'all. I didn't even prepare his baby room until after he was born. It stayed filled with boxes and a half-put-together crib in a cold corner. Every day I passed his room, I would spend energy crying over the child I would never get to meet instead of praying prayers and hopes for what could be. I was swallowed up in thoughts that I would hold a lifeless baby in my arms the day I met him. I began to live not by the hope of what can be, but in fear of what-ifs. What-ifs steal our hope, and they drive a wedge in our relationship with Joy. Let me state that again. If you haven't heard a single word about what to take away from this story, lean in with every effort to understand what I just said. What-ifs steal our hope, and they drive a wedge in our relationship with Joy. Without hope, we look to the future in fear.

But Joy doesn't fear the what-ifs. She thrives on *what can be.*

If the focus of your thought life is on all the things in your future that could go wrong, you will never experience the freedom to live joyfully in the present. I cannot tell you how many stories I have heard from people wishing they could have a positive outlook on life and walk daily in deep-rooted joy and yet who live in fear of something that may or may not ever come to be. I get it. Very personally, I know what it is like to hear the bad report. I know what it is like to get the phone call that someone you cannot replace has been diagnosed with cancer. In my own life, I know what it's like to lose the job. I understand standing in the charity line just so you can give your children school supplies, medicine, or baby formula. I realize how it feels to expect to give birth to death . . . quite literally. And I know the misery of dreading the days ahead in fear of the worst outcome. But I have also since learned the beauty in hoping for the best. When most say, "*Don't* get your hopes up!" I have discovered that I can push back with defiant joy that says, "I *must* get my hopes up!"

Joy doesn't shut down expectations altogether just because it may be better to not be disappointed. Joy allows us to live in *every* emotion life has to offer. She offers courage in the waiting, the hoping, the poverty, the bad report, the regrets. Joy reminds you there's more to this life than living constrained to doubt and resigning to worry. So, go ahead, by all means, get your hopes up. Even if it's just a tiny bit higher than the day before. I have learned the contentment found in the small victories of just getting out of bed, putting pants on, and making it through a day without cussing anyone out. Count those small victories everywhere you can. Celebrate them. Hope begins here in the little things.

I carried regret inside for a season after meeting my son, Duncan. However, I can tell you that regret was suffocated quickly with every new day that I got to hold and care for him. Each time I saw his personality come alive and sweet nuances emerge, I would grow fonder of my son, my little guy, my buddy—the complete boy version of myself. Goodness. Some days I cannot contain the love I have for him. I am reduced to tears even as I retell the story.

Duncan never knew the disconnect I felt while I carried him. He has only known that I am his momma and would do anything in the world to see him happy and healthy and maturing. And you've never met more of a momma's boy than this kid. Sheesh. He never refuses to 'nuggle. (Yes,

I said 'nuggle. It's so special, we drop the *s*.) He lingers in the kitchen just to be near me as I cook or do dishes. He's my forever Valentine date. That's right. He opens my doors, puts our name on the waiting list when we walk in the restaurant, and pays for my meal with the money (courtesy of Dad) in his Spider-Man wallet. Duncan does this every Valentine's Day while my husband does the same for our daughter. If he could, Duncan would walk on water for his momma. To think, I wasted effort and energy fearing the what-ifs when I could have been dreaming in joy about what I now know.

Some of you are just now getting acquainted with Joy. Some of you are beginning to feel that tug on your heart to dream and hope again for what can be. I want to empower you to leave fear behind. There's an incredible quote I found years ago on the internetwebs. Actress and singer Lillian Russell once said, "We all have fear of the unknown. What one does with that fear will make all the difference in the world." If you're ever gonna feel the need to kick something to the curb in your pursuit of Joy, may it be fear! There's nothing more debilitating or detrimental to hope (which we now know is vital to knowing Joy) than fear.

Need still more empowerment and encouragement to leave fear behind in the dust? How about this phenomenal quote from speaker and business coach Stephanie Melish? "Fear is an idea-crippling, experience-crushing, success-stalling inhibitor inflicted only by yourself."

You may be one fear away from experiencing pure joy in your daily life. Call it out. Bring it to the forefront of your thoughts and render it powerless. I didn't do that while I was expecting my son. Since then, I have faced different obstacles that could provoke me to fear the future. Each time, I pause and remember the lesson learned from the friendship and relationship I now have with Duncan. I refuse to allow fear to steal my joy from a single day. I have a choice every day to move away from the what-ifs and embrace why-not. I urge you to start doing the same.

Instead of lingering on what-ifs that are never guaranteed, why not trust and hope in the best that can become?

Instead of letting fear hold you back, why not let hope expand the horizons of your future?

This joy quest doesn't mean we have to fake feeling fine with the future. Not for a single second. But it does allow us to live more abundantly. Abundant life means we may laugh more, yes. It also means we may cry more and feel more deeply than we ever imagined possible. Life abundant means embracing it all as it comes—the good, the bad, the unknown, and the in-between. One thing it doesn't do is feed off fear or cave under assumptions of the worst. If you're hungry for this abundant life and for the joy that is part of it, remove the what-ifs and hope for what can be.

Joy is here for the taking. Why not leave the fear behind and let her take the lead?

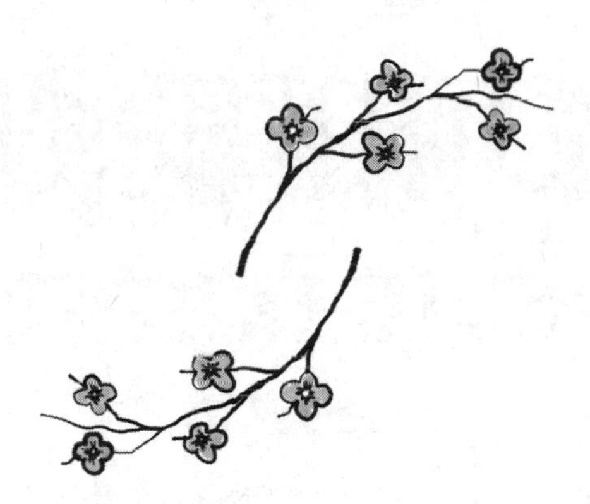

Joy
is
CONTENT
WHETHER
OR
BACK
STAGE
center
STAGE.

Chapter 7

BACKSTAGE, CENTER STAGE, OR WHATEVS

I've never felt more pressure and stress than the night I walked the red carpet at the Country Music Television awards. It was only weeks after I had come home from my whirlwind media, Facebook, and Lucasfilm tour, and now I had been invited to the CMT awards to be a bit in the opening monologue. For a girl who at one point had dreamed of being a regular on *Saturday Night Live*, being a "bit" didn't bother me at all. Nevertheless, I was still stressed. And not by the kind you might naturally assume. I have one word to summarize it all. Are you ready? SPANX. Y'all. I had no need of Spanx ever before in the thirty-seven years I'd spent walking, living, and breathing on this planet until that summer night in Nashville, Tennessee. But that was before the dress.

I had gone to a local plus-sized women's fashion store, tried on everything under $100 that looked pretty, and found this beautiful hot-pink dress with a missing shoulder. Why they didn't give me both shoulders for that price, I will never understand. Oh, fashion, you are an ever-elusive mystery to me!

Either way, it was pretty, popped with color like my bright and bubbly self, and, along with a black shrug to cover the missing shoulder, was within my budget. When I went to the counter to pay, the cashier asked an important question that blindsided me: "Did you need any undergarments to go with this today?" "Uh, like panties and a bra?" I said. "'Cause I have those on now. Wait. Did it look like I wasn't wearing any?" She let out a boisterous chuckle (my kind of person, right there) and pointed me to a rack on the wall lined with Spanx. I asked why I needed flesh-colored bicycle shorts under my dress. Cue a much louder chuckle. She apparently didn't realize I was asking in all seriousness. I went along with the comic timing as though I were lighting up the stage at an open-mic night at the improv. The cashier was obviously a good saleswoman because I left with all things Spanx that I could imagine.

I checked into the hotel in Nashville with a suitcase of sundries I had never possessed before. After showering, I went to try on these miracle undergarments that would suck in and smooth the fluffy rolls around my midsection. I knew if this truly worked, I would forever nickname Spanx "Wonder Panties." Now, apparently, there's an unspoken trick to putting on these bad boys. And I had broken one cardinal rule that I wasn't aware of: Never put them on while slightly damp. Thank the Lord in the high heavens above there isn't hidden camera footage of this moment in the annals of time. You would have thought I was doing a wild interpretive dance trying to get into those fantastic elastics. I mean, I didn't even know if I put it in the right spot or not. *Should I have tucked in my side boob like that?* The struggle was more than real, but I was gonna look smoking hot regardless.

After getting dressed and being whisked downstairs to a lady who painted my face using an array of makeup palettes, I stood in line with a paper in hand that said, "Candace Payne, Chewbacca Mom" to identify myself to the long line of press and expensive cameras.

As I began to look down the media line, I noticed I was standing an arm's length away from several of my past and current celebrity crushes. These aren't crushes you dream about dating or making out with. These are friendship crushes in which you wish and hope for one moment alone at a coffee shop or a good Mexican restaurant over chips and queso.

Along the line, I would stop and be photographed by a hound of camera people asking me to smile and look directly at them. In between photo ops, journalists and reporters asked me questions about my whirlwind experience and viral video. And then, as I awaited the next circuit of interviews, I began to mingle with my pop culture crushes.

I found myself embracing Sadie Robertson as though we'd been lifelong buddies, taking selfies with Vince Vaughn, and chatting in a stolen three-minute conversation with Pharrell Williams about the beauty of the joy that emerged from my inner voice through the Chewbacca mask.

I had practiced walking to my seat before the live show began and got a sneak peek of Keith Urban practicing for his incredible performance. There was a legal-size piece of paper with my face and name taped to the back of the chair where I would sit. I noticed down the row was more names of pop culture icons that I would have never imagined being in the same room with, let alone seated next to for a live taping of an award show. Not only that, I got to hold the sweet and precious, Instagram-famous Doug the Pug. I may need to get the name of his groomer. I have never held a pug more fluffy, soft, and pleasant smelling.

That night was one of the most surreal moments of my life. There was a green room with trays and trays of tiny finger foods. No credit card or cash required. Well, at least, I hope not. I had more than my fair share of them. I enjoyed the evening like it was my last, soaking in every conversation with celebrities and artists between commercial breaks. Shoot, Sadie Robertson and I shared a bucket of popcorn laced with M&M candies. I didn't want the night or the experience to end. And it didn't have to . . . I was given a golden ticket to the after party!

Aside from the rehearsed meetups, I was now invited to peer-mingle with all the celebrity crushes I had longed to meet. I walked around inside a small club that began filling up with people pressing together like a can of sardines. Sad to say, my practical, whirlwind-tired momma self was getting quite exhausted. After about two hours of floating from conversation to conversation on feet that were begging to be freed from the new confines of cute shoes with heels, I headed back to my hotel room, falling asleep still pinching myself to make sure all of this was not just a dream.

With my family at work and school, I flew home the next morning and walked into an empty house with lights off. However, I also walked into an unmistakable smell. Every momma knows this scent. You walk into your home, and something isn't quite right. You begin to sniff out where the odor is hiding.

That day, the culprit was found in my ornery pug Opal's dog crate with her. As I opened the crate door, I saw she had thrown up everywhere. Let's just stop here for a second. Is there not a more alarming sound to wake you in the middle of the night than your dog gagging? I don't know about you, but I could sleep through a tornado tearing apart my ceiling. However, if I faintly hear my dog gag from nine rooms removed, I will jump out of bed and sprint down the hall to try to get Opal outside. There is nothing I hate more than cleaning up dog vomit. It's one thing to clean up and attend to your kids when they're ill. I have the empathy and care that every momma has even in the grossest moments of cleaning up after their sicknesses. However, with a dog, you never know what you will find in their throw-up. Why is there grass in there? Is that a Lego? Y'all. Ick.

So this was my grand welcome-back-to-reality party right on the heels of the most surreal night in the history of the life of Candace Payne. Red carpet to dog vomit, y'all. Just like that.

I muttered aloud as I cleaned Opal's crate, "Why, yes. Yes, I did just side hug and shake hands with Keith Urban last night. And now I'm back to reality. Why is the color orange? It's always orange. Opal, I bet Doug the Pug never throws up in his crate. Why can't you be more like him?" That's right. I even give my poor dog the mom guilt sometimes. Don't judge. We've all done it from time to time. We talk, and somehow our mother escapes our mouths. I know what you probably think as you read this right now: so very glamorous is the life of Chewbacca Mom. It was then I asked myself the question most of us frequently ask ourselves: *Who am I?*

Isn't it funny how often we find our identity in what we do or achieve in our greatest moments? I mean, when I try describing who I am to someone I meet for the first time, I list the highlights of my life. I rarely pitch the moments that I empty the two-day-old-rotten-chicken-smelling trash, discuss the adult acne I had to fight that morning with a pore-cleaning face mask, or discourse about how I often find myself running to and from place to place hauling around tiny humans to activities and lives much more involved than my own. When we describe ourselves, we report in snapshots of our best moments, hoping that the sum of them will become who we truly are. We paint the center-stage highlights and trust people will attribute these successes to our amazing character.

Even when we don't describe ourselves to anyone else, we tend to struggle internally with our identities being wrapped up with what we do instead of who we are. The problem with such thinking is that we begin to believe that we find our worth in what we do day to day instead of who we are at the core of our being. Effortlessly, this can and will more than likely lead to discontent or prideful thinking.

We forget that what we do with our days (glamorous or not) is already an extension of what we value. I know I can walk a red carpet, meet celebrities, and have meaningful talks with them because I value people. I love meeting and making new friends. I love and honor others regardless of their fame or famine. That is at the core of my character because I have decided it's important to be a woman who passionately and furiously loves others regardless of status. I can also come home and clean up dog vomit because I have chosen to develop a heart that longs to serve. Internally, I deliberately work on being a woman who wants to serve others more than I am served. It is a core characteristic of who I long to be when no one is looking. I long to have integrity and a heart that chooses love over arguing, complaining, and blame. I try with every effort to cultivate the kind of character I aspire to and ground my worth in that, rather than letting my worth be defined by my opportunities. Inward character trumps outward opportunity every time, and I want to cultivate the kind of character I can be proud of whether I'm backstage, center stage, or when no one is looking at all.

Joy knows this so well. She lives in every moment fully content. I am not suggesting Joy doesn't aspire to great moments and highlights that would "ooh and awe" the crowds. I am suggesting, though, that she also aims to live in the moments that get thrown on the cutting room floor. Joy knows that the secret of being content is found in being fully satisfied with who you are when no one is looking, no matter what role you are living.

As I mentioned briefly earlier, there was a season in my late teens and early twenties when all I wanted to do was be a cast member or special guest on the television show *Saturday Night Live*. I had grown up watching *SNL* every Saturday night and remember its sketch comedy and parody offering weekly levity to any circumstance in which we found ourselves. Some of my favorite characters were Wayne and Garth from a sketch called Wayne's World, the church lady as performed by Dana Carvey, the awkward Spartan cheerleaders (Will Ferrell and Cheri Oteri), and my all-time personal favorite, Chris Farley as the motivational speaker Matt Foley. I not only would watch and laugh along with my family, but I began writing sketch ideas to perform for my eclectic collection of stuffed animals and Cabbage Patch kids. I also remember trying out for all the plays in high school. And even if the character I was cast as was incredibly solemn, I would find a way to turn the role toward comic relief . . . unintentionally. I dreamed of bringing people the same laughter that I enjoyed on *SNL* while living in that single-wide trailer.

The desire that I had to be on *Saturday Night Live* was so intense, I would do anything and everything to get there. After high school, I ventured to open mic nights at stand-up comedy clubs and even created, held auditions, and traveled for a short stint with my very own improvisational acting group. *Saturday Night Live* wasn't just a goal for me; it was where I believed I would find my purpose and identity.

Now, not a single one of you reading this book first heard of me from my glory days as a cast member or special guest on *SNL*. Nah, that dream still waits in the wings. (Don't think for a second I have forgotten it.) However, there came a moment when my striving for that gig had to end. Through circumstances beyond my control, I abruptly ended my college studies to move back home and care for ailing grandparents. During that season, I met my husband, married, and put many dreams on hold to pursue family and love. I entered into anonymous years backstage, as it were. I no longer found myself in the audition line trying out for roles but in the grocery checkout line buying bulk diapers. And to say I didn't struggle would be untrue. For a while, it felt as though my purpose and identity were fading like the late-day sun.

The shift came when I realized who I was in the quiet of every moment wasn't dependent on what stage I was on. You see, as I was caring for my grandmother struggling with Alzheimer's and dementia, she would often laugh at my jokes. Annie Mae was someone special to me. More than my grandma, she was a beautiful mirror into everything kind and lovely that I longed to become. Both before and after the dementia took hold of her, she was an ornery lady with sass and sparkle in her eyes in equal parts. You never truly knew what that woman was plotting. In her younger days, my grandma would make the best pot roast, force me to take a nap when I visited her house, eat a five-gallon bucket of ice cream in one sitting if she wanted (she loved pecans, pralines, and cream), and jerk out her dentures in one swift motion to scare the dickens out of me for her own sheer amusement.

In her latter days, Annie Mae didn't even remember my name. Still, I knew she *knew* me. When together and humming hymns as I brushed her hair, I felt more love and appreciation than I could ever earn on a stage. In those quiet moments and lost memories, I found contentment in just being her granddaughter, in simply sitting and holding her hand. No applause or crowd laughter will ever hold as much weight as the memories I have of making my sweet Annie Mae laugh. We often assume that contentment is a unique trait that people either innately have or have not. I was convinced for years that you were just a special person if you lived with contentment. However, since then, I have disproved that lie over and over again. Contentment is very much a learned behavior and response. It's a choice about how we react to the world around us.

The beautiful old hymn "It Is Well with My Soul" was one of my favorites to hear my grandma sing while I was growing up.

The hymn writer, Horatio G. Spafford, was a successful lawyer and businessman in Chicago with a lovely family—a wife, Anna, and five children. However, they were not strangers to tears and tragedy. A young son died of scarlet fever in 1871, and in that same year, much of their business was lost in the Great Chicago Fire. However, he rebuilt his business to be successful once more in the following years.

In November 1873, the French ocean liner *Ville du Havre* left the New York Harbor for Europe with 313 passengers aboard. Among the passengers were Mrs. Spafford and their four daughters. Although Mr. Spafford had planned to go with his family, he found it necessary to stay in Chicago to help solve an unexpected business problem. Planning to travel on another ship, he told his wife he would join her and their children in Europe a few days later.

A week into the ocean crossing, the *Ville du Havre* collided with a powerful, iron-hulled Scottish ship, the *Loch Earn*. Suddenly, all of those on board were in grave danger. Anna hurriedly brought her four children to the deck. Kneeling there with Annie, Maggie, Bessie, and Tanetta, she prayed that God would spare them if that was His will, or to make them willing to endure whatever awaited them.

Within twelve minutes, the *Ville du Havre* slipped beneath the dark waters of the Atlantic, carrying with it 226 of the passengers, including the four Spafford children. A sailor, rowing a small boat over the spot where the ship went down, spotted a woman floating on a piece of the wreckage.

It was Anna, still alive. He pulled her into the boat, and they were picked up by another large vessel which, nine days later, landed in Cardiff, Wales. From there she wired her husband a message which began, "Saved alone, what shall I do?" Mr. Spafford later framed the telegram and placed it in his office.

Another of the ship's survivors, Pastor Weiss, later recalled Anna saying, "God gave me four daughters. Now they have been taken from me. Someday I will understand why."

Mr. Spafford booked passage on the next available ship and left to join his grieving wife. As the ship reached the vicinity where the *Ville du Havre* sank, the captain called Spafford to his cabin and told him they were over the place where his children had been lost. According to Bertha Spafford Vester, a daughter born after the tragedy, Horatio Spafford wrote "It Is Well with My Soul" while on this journey.

You have to look at these lyrics. They are utterly powerful, poignant, and heart-wrenching.

Verse One:

When peace, like a river, attendeth my way,
When sorrows like sea billows roll,
Whatever my lot, thou hast taught me to say,
It is well, it is well with my soul.

Chorus:

It is well with my soul,
It is well, it is well with my soul.

How can this kind of contentment with life even be possible? How can one even sing while in the midst of tragedy and disappointment? How? I propose this: It is learned. Contentment is not a natural response. It doesn't fit. It goes against the grain. Found within such a heart—a heart that's content regardless of tragedy, heartache, disappointment, rejection, or failure—is my beautiful friend, Joy. She may not always be full of laughter, but she most assuredly is full of comfort when we know who we are in spite of our circumstances or position in life.

I'd like to say I am a very well-learned student on this subject. (Did you appreciate my humility here as well? Sheesh. You get the point.) Y'all. It's a daily struggle to detach my identity, who I am at the core, from my successes or failures. Countless times I fall into the trap of thinking my identity is somehow better or worse depending on the spotlight or the lack thereof. It's a daily task to remember that I am more than the sum of my moments, that my identity is not based on or limited to my highlight reel.

After the Chewbacca Mom video went viral, I spent flashes of time in rooms with people whom I long admired and fawned over like a teenager with a crush. As much as those moments are astounding for what they are, do you want to know what makes me feel the most joy as I look upon that year of chance meetings? I look at how content I was when I came home to dog puke. I've told you how much I love-love cleaning up dog puke, yet my heart was content and grateful to be home that day. Whether sitting alone in my living room or on a carpool karaoke set with James Corden and J. J. Abrams, I am learning to know who I am apart from the daily moments or tasks at hand. And it's not at all easy. There's much to learn about yourself when you begin to look within.

Another perk of learning contentment is what Joy offers alongside. She holds out a beautifully wrapped package when we learn to respond with contentment instead of worry or performance.

What's in the box? What is this beautiful gift? It's a free pass from pressure. The one thing I love the most about my relationship with Joy is the acceptance I feel when I am with her. The pressure's off. *You're off the hook!* Has anyone ever told you that? Have you ever truly experienced what it is like to be free from pressure to perform? As I was learning and am still learning to be content in all circumstances, I find that who I am is enough.

I am so grateful for how the world found me. Are you kidding? All those years of auditions and preparation for *Saturday Night Live*, wanting to bring laughter and levity to a hurting world, were ultimately outdone by a simple four-minute selfie wearing a child's toy mask. I didn't turn on the Facebook Live video to gain the attention of millions or land the dream spot on *SNL* (though I wouldn't turn it down; Lorne Michaels, I'm talking to you). I turned it on to share the joy with my friends and family. I was comfortable in who I was at that moment when I heard the call to play. I was content with the fact that I was a momma wanting a break from the chaos of running errands. I was reveling in simple joys that are hidden in the most mundane of days.

There wasn't a gleam of performance in my eye. I was content. And if there's something I am learning for sure, it is that Contentment is a cousin to Joy.

The question "Who am I?" becomes more settled every day when I give pause to remember who I am backstage, center stage, or whatevs. To go from obscurity to popularity overnight, it'd be easy to lose sight of that. So, who am I? Am I Candace Payne, the stay-at-home mom of two and wife of one? Or am I "Chewbacca Mom," the Facebook Live record-breaker? I'm both. And I'm content to be both. We are far more than the one-dimensional pictures our highlight reel could ever show, and that is a very good thing.

I don't know about you, but I have always loved *The Lion King*. And I especially love what it has to say about claiming our true identity.

In this film, we happen upon the coronation of a future king, the infant lion cub Simba. He is born of royalty and sings his heart out about how he "just can't wait to be king." However, his uncle, Scar, plots to usurp Simba's rightful position as king by assassinating Simba's father, Mufasa. Scar stokes fear in a gullible Simba by blaming him for the untimely death of his father and tells him to run away from his destiny and hide forever in shame and fear.

Through a series of somewhat fortunate events, Simba finds unlikely jungle friends and adopts a new philosophy of life: Hakuna Matata. It means, in a nutshell, don't worry, be happy. It's his "problem-free philosophy."

However, this extreme freedom from personal responsibility goes directly against who Simba was created to become. He was never made to ignore or escape his problems in obscurity. He was, by design, the king of the jungle and the Pride Lands. He was a lion, for heaven's sake, destined to lead! Yet there he was, without a care in the world, giving up on it all.

Under an illusion and lie to his true identity, Simba had resorted to abandoning his throne—and all responsibility with it—and living on bugs and worms, which I shouldn't have to remind you, lions are not made to do.

In the years of running from who he was, Simba embraced a lie that he was the sum of his failures—that is, until his father Mufasa visited him in a vision. Mufasa comes with a thunderous reminder to Simba: "You have forgotten who you are, and so forgotten me. Remember who you are."

Because that scene always resonated with me something fierce when I would feel intense insecurity about who I was in life or what I was doing with my days, just a couple of months after the Chewbacca Mom whirlwind began, I decided to create very permanent reminders to stay in the struggle to learn contentment every day. And so, I got two tattoos that I could look at whenever I felt I was losing the battle.

On my left forearm, I had inked the cave rendering of Simba with the words "remember who you are" circling beneath. And on my right forearm is my little happy

Wookiee. You can spy it upside down on the cover of this book. (You didn't realize you bought an eye-spy book as well? Hashtag: BONUS.) Yes, I wanted to mark that moment in my car I had ended up sharing with hundreds of millions of people. But more personally (as you, dear reader, now know), it signifies that I will forever be content, whether backstage, center stage, or whatevs. It's in contentment that I find authentic joy. Every time. It's there I step into my destiny and experience freedom that I can live fully and present in every moment this life gives me, great or small.

What about you? Do you need to remember who you really are—at your essence, at your core? What would it take to remind you?

Listen, I get it. Not everyone finds life-changing symbolism in Simba or Wookiees.

But I bet you can identify with an image or quote or something else that resonates deep within and speaks true to who you are, something that stirs you and motivates you. My advice? Hold on to that. Get creative and find a way to put this truth in front of you every day, and don't let circumstances pull you away from this anchor.

Whether you're backstage, center stage, or whatevs, claim your identity and get comfortable in it, and let this lead you to Joy.

Joy
ALWAYS
TELLS THE
TRUTH.

Chapter 8

QUIT SHOULD-ING YOURSELF

Birthdays have become my personal New Year's Day. I love start-overs, new beginnings, a good deadline. I love meditating on what could be within a few short months of where I currently am. I'm a goal-setter, a visionary by design. Somewhere in my early thirties, I got the idea that it would serve me best to make all my goals, resolutions, and ambitions on the day I was entering a clean-slate year.

Birthdays are a great start-again date. It's the first day of being however old you are for the very first time . . . each year. How cool is that? I loved my personal reset day being different than the rest of humanity's. I didn't have to entertain inquiries on what I did or didn't plan for the new year from even the most unlikely people. Does the cashier at the super store really need to know if I'm going to join a gym or not? Did she need to assume I was on a health kick just because I bought new stretchy pants (to accommodate bloating after overeating) that just so happen to be called yoga pants as well? No. No, she didn't. So, I resolved to create a secret day to plot and plan personal improvements.

I always had a habit of making New Year's resolutions that were nearly impossible to keep. So, what if I set a goal I knew I couldn't help but keep? A goal that was actually reachable and not a long shot. For me, the options were limited to my faithful ventures. So, I jokingly resolved to eat a taco once a day the entire year I turned thirty-five. I mean, surely I could keep that one because I was already doing it unintentionally. It was awesome. Tacos. Every. Day. (The good thing about tacos is you can eat whatever you like, just as long as it has a shell of some sort. Easy. I can't tell you how many times I made Chinese fried rice night an Asian taco night. Shoot. I even wrapped a slice of lasagna inside a corn tortilla. Not bad. Don't knock it till you try it.)

I am not one who usually likes to set health goals because I, like many of you, have set them only to quit them within mere weeks. Shoot, I had even given up on a resolution the very next morning when my thighs screamed, "Help me, Jesus!" as I tried to sit on the toilet after my stair-climbing workout. New Year's Day resolutions aren't really my thing. Turns out, keeping them isn't either.

However, only days before my thirty-sixth birthday, I was challenged to think about my vision of what I wanted to accomplish and who I wanted to be the following year. Now, this wasn't a one-on-one conversation. My pastor proclaimed this challenge to a roomful of people. I was just one of them, but it may as well have translated to a coffee shop talk with him staring me straight in the eyes. Of course, he had no way of knowing it was about to be my personal New Year's Day. However, it felt serendipitous of him to ask. So, right then and there, I closed my eyes and asked myself a simple question: "What is it I'm meant to do this year?"

We've all asked ourselves about our purpose: who we truly are and why we are alive. Somehow, this moment was different. Different because it was the first time I had listened to the response with an open heart. Before, I had often shut down anything that didn't mirror what I was already passionate about or doing on a regular basis that I could just amp up to the next level.

For example, if I were decent at playing guitar and writing songs, I might sign up to mentor other songwriters. A simple variation and, yes, still a challenge. But I wasn't setting any new goals that would afford me the lessons learned through failure. My list would reflect the things I was already skilled at doing but hadn't mastered. This time, though, there was a tug on my heart to add to my resolutions something that was foreign to my natural talents and skill sets. I felt unsettled in my gut that I hadn't pushed myself the year before when I claimed my victorious year of taco indulgence . . . and it wasn't just the tacos talking. It was an empty celebration that left me craving more than the minimal effort I could offer. I longed for a real challenge, to feel victorious over something which I had actually wrestled and defeated.

If you've followed me online at all, you soon discovered

after the Chewbacca Mom video, there was more talent within my voice than the laugh heard around the world. I am a singer, a communicator, and now an author. Real friends who have known me for years know that I am also an illustrator, artist, crochet hooker (yes, that's the term . . . and, no, I haven't put it on a T-shirt just yet), songwriter, and musician.

When people find out my bag of artistic skills, they often ask, more as a compliment, "Is there anything you *can't* do?" And I developed a canned response in an attempt to be funny. "Yeah, there's a lot I can't do. If it's athletic in nature, you name it, I suck at it." I don't excel at mountain climbing, hikes in the woods, rappelling, tennis, soccer, or softball. I mean, I've even lost a game of tetherball while playing myself. And I sure as heaven don't ever attempt to run unless I am being chased by a large mammal that could kill me. Y'all. I know my limitations. Well, at least I thought I did. But as I closed my eyes to ask what year thirty-seven would look like, that tug I was feeling on my heart was whispering a new challenge. In my mind's eye, I saw my feet in a pair of orange running shoes hitting the pavement in slow motion as I heard a still, small voice say, "Candace, this year you're gonna be a runner."

At first, I wanted to form that whisper into a million figurative scenarios that were attainable without failure. To be honest, I did. There's a Scripture passage that speaks about being renewed by hoping in God. It eloquently states, "They [who hope in the Lord] will soar on wings like eagles; they will run and not grow weary; they will walk and not be faint." Because I had heard the quote so often, I naturally assumed it's what this vision of running in orange shoes meant. I mean, seriously. I was not about to go out and buy a pair of orange tennis shoes and swap out tacos for kale, granola, and daily runs at five in the morning.

Certainly, this vision meant that I was going to face some obstacles and successfully overcome them, not that I would actually have to get my butt off the couch and run. Win, win. Yeah. Not so much. I couldn't get over the internal struggle that my interpretation was cheating, and worst of all, cheating myself of something great awaiting me in my future.

I gave pause to the idea that I could be a runner. I didn't focus on what it meant to run or all the logistics of downloading the latest app to remind me to run or make a calendar game plan. Instead, I asked myself why I was so resistant to this vision. Why was I so quick in my opposition? That was a harder task than just getting off my butt and running. I hadn't spent much effort looking within, to wonder why I always tended to rule out things that would or could benefit me. I had done this with many things in my life, not just physical exertion. I had created a long list of activities that I felt were not for me, or were too hard for me. It was a list of statements I conveniently used to count myself out before I even tried something new. Statements such as:

- I'm not a runner.
- I'm not athletic.
- I'm not the pretty girl.

- I'm not an ab model. (This one is hard to believe, I know.)
- I'm not the girl who wears makeup all the time.
- I'm not girly.
- I don't get my nails and hair done unless it's prom, a wedding, or I meet the president (which I have never done, but I assume you'd need beautifully manicured nails if you did).
- I don't go swimming in public because I don't show my body in a swimsuit. (And, to be honest? I hadn't even owned a legitimate swimsuit in years. I kept buying athletic, breathable clothing that would cover from upper chest to mid-thigh when I'd swim.)
- I am not the girl who attracts others by her beauty.
- I don't lift weights.
- I don't jump rope, do jumping jacks, or give cause for my boobs to bounce in public.
- I don't put myself in situations that would cause me to sweat. (Fat people are judged as having poor hygiene when they constantly sweat. I even avoid eating too much steak in any given setting in fear of developing the "meat sweats.")
- I do not worry about things such as carb counting or calorie intake. (I will always be a fluffy and bigger woman. I was born that way.)
- I don't have a voice that matters to the masses.
- I'm not a public speaker. (I was comfortable using my gifts of singing and playing guitar for a crowd, but I

never had the desire to open up. Who am I with words that aren't scripted or comedic?)

- I'm not smart. (I went to more elementary schools than I could keep count of and felt as though my educational foundation left me shaky, to say the least.)
- I don't know how to spell words and often overuse the same adjective for everything when I find one I like. (Have you heard me speak before in an interview? I am on strict personal lockdown from using the word *insane* more than two times in five minutes.)
- I'm not a writer. (If you can't see the irony in this one by now, reading chapter eight in a book I authored, I think you may need to look up the definition of *irony*. I did. Seriously. Right before typing this sentence. It fits. Whew!)

This isn't a definitive list. There are more items I could add. Some I know well; they govern how I spend my life. Others, I'm still learning. It's amazing to uncover the lies we tell ourselves daily. I have so many boundaries that I keep in place because I've told myself that I am not, I cannot, or I will not. If you asked, I could recall events that shaped my list. I know these ideas didn't just pop up out of the blue. I remember hurtful words from crushes I had developed. I remember the rejection and failure I faced in competitive sports. I can even recollect moments where I physically could not keep up with my peers. I also remember participating in weight loss programs as a third grader. I was never able to climb the rope in gym class. And then there was the dreaded day they would weigh you in front of everyone else and call out your weight to the record taker holding the clipboard. (I've never felt more embarrassment than as a fifth grader weighing in at one hundred fifty-one pounds. For a nine-year-old, that is the definition of obesity, and the humiliation of hearing it aloud stained a memory that cannot easily be wiped clean.)

And now, I found myself at a crossroads, with a list of fallacies playing repeatedly in my brain about who I was because of those moments. At this juncture, I knew I was either going to live another year believing I *was* all those limitations—or defy the list.

The first step to defying the repetitive lies swirling in my head was to confess my goal to someone I trusted. Often when you speak something aloud, it becomes real and solidified in your mind—and I wanted this resolution to be real. I told a longtime girlfriend that I was going to start walking (running?) every day. It was a somewhat small, doable goal, and when I spoke it aloud, I knew that there was no turning back. This goal had come to life. This friend is one who jumps onboard wherever you are in life and champions whatever new crazy cause or adventure you pursue. (Everyone needs a friend like this.) I didn't reveal the list of negatives. I spun it as a random risk in the ever-changing life of Candace. I doubt she knew how intense a journey I was about to embark on. And I didn't want her to know . . . not just yet. If I'm honest, I was afraid. I knew I could have a huge victory on the other side of this moment . . . or a huge failure. I didn't want to disappoint myself, and I didn't want deep questions to push me too far too quick.

How many times do we do this in relationships that could serve us well? How many times do we only share the glossy side and never expose the dirt? I knew I was doing myself a disservice, but I still had my list lying to me that I was weak. If I voiced my audacious goal out loud, I knew it would become more real, and there would be no turning back. So, I played it off the best I could to my sweet friend: that I was just trying something new and was going to begin walking.

With this newfound knowledge, my bestie gave me a fun birthday gift. She knew if I was going to start walking and/or running, I needed the right shoes. Soon after, a box arrived on my porch from an online store. Inside was an adorable pair of pink and gray running shoes. (Admit it. You were secretly hoping they'd be orange. I was too.) I sat down to try them on, but they didn't fit. Usually, I would have taken this as a sign, or rather an excuse, that I did not need to begin running; that my imagination was the only thing running . . . running wild, that is. However, this friend means the world to me, so I let her know I was going to exchange them and that I would, in fact, use them.

So, one day I did something I'd never done before: I walked into a store that only sold athletic footwear. Did you even know they made such places? Well, they do. I was intimidated, and a bit overwhelmed. I went to the nearest employee sporting a referee whistle and a gold name badge and begged for wisdom in deciding on a good pair of running shoes.

He asked what kind of running I planned to do. Are you serious? What *kind* of running? Call me a simpleton, but I had no clue there were multiple types of running, let alone the need for different things on your feet to do them. I was in over my head and wanted to hightail it out of there immediately. Instead, I did what I do best by embracing the awkward moments, and confessed I had no clue what he was asking.

There is such freedom when you embrace what you don't know and acknowledge your shortcomings. You don't have to have your act together all the time. Some of the most liberating moments in my life were confessing things I didn't know.

The salesman began pulling box after box from the shelf, shoes with different types of soles and heel shapes. I discovered I liked the feel of lighter shoes compared to those with a thicker sole. We finally narrowed our search to three pairs. There was one white and gray pair that felt particularly amazing as I hobbled one-shoe-on-one-shoe-off down the aisle. The only problem was that they didn't appear to have my exact size and width in stock. So, the ever-helpful whistle-wearing employee said a girl's favorite shopping words: "Let me go check in the back."

Five minutes later, he returned with a closed box. He warned me that he had found the right shoe; it just wasn't the right color. As he opened the box, I saw a tiny hint of orange. The more he pulled back the lid, the more I felt goosebumps rise from the center of the spine at the base of my neck and top of my shoulders, and then spread like an outbreak all over my body. Those weren't just orange shoes. No. They were the *exact* orange shoes I had seen in my mind. They even had the nod of yellow stitching and black woven details that I didn't even remember them having until I saw them "live" in the hands of a stranger.

Never had I experienced the shoe-shopping joy that women speak of until that moment. I decided to "just do it" (pun intended) and use this shoe as the exchange for my girlfriend's sweet birthday gift. I was so excited to take them home and start using them.

Know this: I am still no expert on running or walking. And I didn't want any unsolicited advice on how to become a pro, either, because the physicality of this new habit wasn't even half the picture. No, I wanted to do the real work: breaking down strongholds in my mind that were limiting my life.

Every time I would begin to walk, I would recite my list internally. I would muse over just one item at a time. Otherwise, I would have been severely overwhelmed. I started with the obvious: Why did I tell myself I couldn't run?

It was a simple question. But it was an act of resistance, challenging my tendency to count myself out before I had even tried. That's the power of why.

Why had I told myself I wasn't a runner? It was more

than facing rejection or comparing my lack of skill to the junior-high track star. I could see that I had two working legs, breath in my lungs, and that running was no threat to my health. The reason I started lying to myself was rooted much deeper, and this question led to questioning everything on my list. To uncover the answers, I needed time alone with my thoughts—which I got as I walked each morning. I had decided I was going to walk often and run (even if it was only in fifteen-second sprints) every day.

Each day I would lace up my orange running shoes and leave the front porch of my home feeling a calm and peace that I had tried to gain in my thoughts for years. It's as if every step I took was stomping out tiny remnants of campfires of deceptions I had long believed. As a person who earnestly intends to grow my relationship with God, I would use this time to pray, talking with my God about my list and recalling His words found in the Bible. For every single lie on my list, Scripture countered with a truth. And praying no longer felt as though I was saying words that would hit a short brick ceiling above me. Talking to and listening to that small voice within began to cross out the list of lies one by one. I began feeling such a freedom while walking and running that I didn't want to miss a single day.

That was easy enough before the Chewbacca Mom video went viral. In its aftermath, however, the interviews and travel made it a nightmare to find extra time and places to walk. But I was determined. The walking and running were so essential to honing a new skill of calming my mind and had become such an important routine, I made it a priority no matter where I was or what I was doing. So much so that I found myself running across a grassy knoll atop the Facebook headquarters in California. Yes, you read that right.

The media and press whirlwind was overwhelming, to say the least. Imagine the pressure of never doing interviews or being on live television before, and now the entire world seemed to know your name and wanted you to retell your experience. How would you deal with the overnight success? I didn't have a game plan. I had, however, established a way to center my thoughts. And I knew if I was to keep my head in the midst of the chaos, I was going to make every effort to keep that routine.

A few days after I utilized Facebook's live video platform and became the record holder for most views, I was invited to tour their company headquarters. As I walked through the elaborate campus, two thoughts went back and forth in my mind. The first was amazement at the beauty of the place. Y'all. There's a woodshop (what they make other than keychains and the super sweet plaque they presented me with upon arrival is still a mystery), an incredible restaurant where the whole community dines as though it's the local hot spot, and a park on the roof. I didn't want to miss a single moment of the wonder in each turn, stairwell, and hallway.

However, my other thought was beginning to stifle me and give me cold sweats. I kept repeating to myself, "Who am I? What in the world am I doing here?" As I listened half-intently to the description of how they built this amazing rooftop park, I became inundated with a sense of unworthiness, the same feeling that I was being laughed at that I felt during homecoming week in college. I told myself to shake that garbage from my thoughts. (In my mind, I had Jenny from *Forrest Gump* yelling over the voice of my tour guide, "Run, Forrest, run!")

And then I abruptly interrupted this sweet and tender-voiced millennial. "Hey! I have an idea. Have you ever just run the length of this knoll and back?"

Unmistakably caught off guard from what felt like her scripted tour, she said, "Why do you ask? You wanna do it? You wanna run?"

"Yeah. I do. I think I'm gonna run over there and run right back. Want to join me?"

She took off her high heels, lay them in the grass, and we took off running together. In that four minutes, I recentered. I recalibrated. I embraced and owned those sweat beads running down my forehead while with a group of dashingly thin and beautiful people. As we turned a corner atop the roof, I asked for a few minutes to catch my breath and be alone. I sat in a chair and overlooked miles upon miles of the most gorgeous landscape you can imagine—sparkling water, green treetops, cityscape, and more. It was a clear, blue day and nothing was impeding my view. I had gone from my living room to the top of the world.

I sat there and prayed for a few minutes—words that, to this day, I don't remember. However, I do remember the thought that came to mind as I lifted my eyes to the horizon one more time before rejoining the patient group waiting to escort Chewbacca Mom. I thought: I'm sitting on top of a building that houses some of the most creative minds and concepts in the whole world. As a matter of fact, their motivation is to connect the entire world. They have seemingly unlimited resources and can do the most incredible Willy Wonka-style imaginings to their headquarters. Now, if that's what Facebook can do, what more could a God with unlimited resources do with little ole me? I suddenly felt a charge that I was given grace to connect this world in ways beyond my inherent capabilities. I knew at that moment that I had been given the opportunity not just to share joy but to empower people to live joy-filled lives. For some reason, I felt as though I only heard that acutely because I was obedient to answer the internal call to run . . . to embrace my new identity as a runner. And now I understood that it was both a figurative and a literal title.

Currently, I am on a quest to abolish the list of can'ts I have believed about myself. One common obstacle consistently rears its ugly head when I consider changing these thoughts. It's this hideous, offensive word that accompanies my goals. What word, you ask? *Should.* I cannot tell you how many times I shame myself or my past or my present struggles with that cuss word. Yes, it indeed has become a cuss word to me.

Here's a small example. I will look in my past with regret on how I allowed myself to become so overweight or lazy or careless with my health. It's in those musings that I hear that

I *should* have done better. I *should* have been more proactive, *should* have made better choices in what I ate and my level of physical activity. Over the years, I've heard this pushy inner voice say I *should* do Tae Bo, Zumba, and Ab Rocking, and buy everything that Suzanne Somers sells on late-night shopping channels.

In my present struggles, I am still tempted to embrace counterfeit joy over authentic joy. Yes, I know. The person who shared four minutes of straight-up joy with millions struggles daily with maintaining authentic joy. It's so easy to hear that little temptation that says I should be happier on days I wake up in a foul mood. But since shutting up the *shoulds*, nothing within me feels pressure to maintain this false platform, because the moment the door was opened to me was one of raw, authentic, and defiant joy. That doesn't mean I won't face the decision to answer Should's call to make do with less just because of the people watching. Every time I hear I should do something outside of the call to be authentic, I know it is an assault on the progress I'm currently making in uncovering what a life full of joy looks like.

That tiny word, *should*, tries desperately to lay claim on my future as well. It divides paths that would otherwise be clear and narrow. It pushes like a bully to work and perform and hold tight to something I have to pour all my power and effort into to maintain.

If you're ever going to break up with the list of lies you possess about yourself, it's not only time, but vital to do so. Today this is my invitation to you: Shut the *should* up!

Come on; somebody needs to read that again. Shut the SHOULD up!

There's beauty in living each and every moment knowing that you can take any path you choose and find each step that is authentic to your story. I'm not telling you to embrace some crazy thinking where you do only what pleases yourself, or that you now have a free pass to live life without a moral compass. Where there is injustice toward others or even yourself, take a stand. But please don't stand just to earn the applause and fleeting popularity of a crowd. Live authentically with the grace to know risks are where bridges of joy are forged over many waters of disappointments, regrets, failures, and lists of can'ts. Loving others and living brightly as a light to a hopeless and hurting world is possible because you *are* enough—even if you're a work in progress. Authentic and defiant joy embraces the fact that it is more than okay but absolutely necessary to quit should-ing yourself.

So, go ahead. Make your list of lies. Pick just one small lie you've believed far too long about yourself. Decide to replace that lie by doing the opposite of the core belief that has held you back. Then do a gutsy thing and tell a friend—name the lie you've been believing and the truth you want to live instead. Have your friend hold you accountable and support you when you feel the desire to embrace the negative.

Be a full-on rebel and prove your lying list wrong! Tackle as many as you can, one-by-one, every single day. When it gets tough, don't be surprised. It means you're close to a breakthrough. Keep at it and don't give up!

Shut the *shoulds* up! Run, Forrest, run! Do what you were made to do. True joy waits on the other side of every small victory.

And the next time that small voice whispers to you about a big dream, believe it—and buckle up for the ride.

Joy
won't let you cry
won't let you cry
alone and she
for long.

Chapter 9

A BOY, HIS JOY, & BUZZ LIGHTYEAR

I have a small confession to make: I never told my kids that Disney World existed because we couldn't afford it. Plain and straightforward. Chris and I had chosen to be a one-income family. We knew that we would only have the first years of our kids' lives one time. Because those moments were so important to us, we chose to sacrifice a few things along the way. One of those things was a family vacation to Disney World, and I began to regret that sacrifice.

Somewhere, packed tightly in a box, with multiple other VHS tapes, there is a video of me at Disney World as a child. I was wearing a souvenir yellow shirt with Mickey Mouse waving "hello" on the front. I also rocked a purple and pink '80s-inspired trucker hat with the purple dragon character Figment dashingly drawn on the top. I don't know if you ever have experienced the greatness that is the ride with Figment at Epcot before. Y'all. I can only describe it as the same way I felt when I first saw the riverboat scene in the movie *Willy Wonka and the Chocolate Factory*. It was altogether frightening and yet magical at the same time. I remember everything about that trip as a child through the lens of wonder and enchantment.

Living as a family that experienced both "feast" and "famine" seasons, memories of vacations were more than mere memories. They were small, sustaining snacks of joy that reminded me why I loved my family even in the most despairing of moments. To this day, I still smile when I think of my brothers spending a whole afternoon talking about how much fun they had on Space Mountain instead of the usual teenage sibling rivalry that ended in someone being called a "butthead" or "idiot." (Those were the best insults they could muster since they were also obsessed with John Hughes's films, which served as their inspiration.)

At Disney World, they were not only nice to each other, but they enjoyed each other, like friends who enjoy each other's company. My sister, who was a teenager when I was still in grade school, would hold my hand as we walked through the theme parks because she (wait for it) *wanted* to! I even remember sharing a chocolate croissant with her at Epcot Center in the small village staged to look like France. If you know how much of a struggle it is to share a room (and for a while, even the same full-size bed) with a little sister who never gives the space you crave, you understand how beautiful and rare these moments were. I was convinced Disney World was more than enchanting. It was truly magical. And I wanted my kids to experience it through their young eyes much as I had when I was near their same ages. However, it remained just a "wish that my heart made" because of the reality of our limited resources.

Two weeks before the Chewbacca Mom video, I was alone in my house pouring out these wants and wishes to God. It wasn't your average prayer time when you're in trouble and promise God you'll never do something wrong again. This time, I was asking God if He even saw me or cared for me.

If you're someone who doesn't believe in God or thinks talking to God might be slightly crazy, I hope you'll hear my heart here—I am not trying to debate your beliefs; I'm just candidly trying to be honest through the lens of mine.

I had placed my faith in God and fully invested in learning to trust Him for all my *needs*. However, I couldn't help but wonder if He cared about my *wants* as well. Did God understand that I had willingly taken a massive pay cut to do what is often the most overlooked and undervalued job in nearly every single culture? As I changed diapers and cleaned up toys and baby food messes from the floor, did He care about the fact that I would never see my children's faces light up when they got to see the wonder that is Disney World?

Even as I start divulging my wants on this page, it feels so trite. I know there are much more dire and pressing prayers. You may be praying far more desperate prayers right now, and that's real.

Yet I felt the need to be utterly honest as I talked with God that day. This was a #nofilter prayer, y'all. I felt unworthy even making my requests known for fear they weren't noble or pressing enough, so I told Him that. Did God care about my wants, even the ones that didn't qualify for the community prayer chain list?

If you struggle with faith, you have already had or will have this thought cross your mind someday. It felt a bit daring, even a bit defiant. And a little scary, too. I mean, are you allowed to ask for so small a thing from such a big God?

I knew God cared about every aspect of my life. At least, that's what I heard each week in my church's worship lyrics and sermons that spoke of God as a good Father and giver of good gifts. But in reality I felt I was getting lumps of spiritual coal in my stocking every time I brought a minor request to His attention.

I was at a crossroads in my faith. Did God earnestly care about me? Did He see that I was trying my hardest to please and love Him, and did He know how I still felt ignored? I had heard it said that God is an extravagant giver. And I want to be very clear here: I wasn't asking God for extravagance to be selfish and gain more stuff to fill a void that can only be satisfied by my genuine relationship with Him. No, it's so much more than that. In my faith journey, I don't want to just know more about God; I want to mirror His goodness. If He is indeed an extravagant giver, how could I be like Him with nothing extravagant to give? How could I address worldwide hurts and needs amid the dirty dishes and loads of laundry of my safe, suburban home, especially when we struggled to keep our own family fed and groceries in the pantry? Out of what "extra" could I show this world extravagant giving? I knew, somewhere in the recesses of my soul, I didn't know this giving aspect of God. So in the spirit of honesty and with plenty of emotion, I asked God to meet not only my needs but honor my wants as well.

I know what some of you are thinking. You're worried God was going to strike me down with lightning right then and there. I was too, a bit. However, I was more concerned with the fact that my faith was so small to believe that God didn't care. I had been spending years asking for what I thought He wanted to hear. In doing so, what I had discovered was that it was nearly as effective as going to a bank with unlimited resources and applying for a five-dollar loan. Here was a huge God that I believe owns the entire universe, but I wouldn't dare ask a bold prayer from Him? Y'all. We don't spoil our children in any respect, but when our kids ask my husband and me for anything, if it's in our power to get it for them, we will move heaven and earth to do so. The necessary provisions we offer daily without them ever asking for them. When they come to us with wants, we have many times rearranged or saved or given out of the desire to see them happy.

My voice shook as I began to pray, "God, if You truly are a giver of every good and perfect gift, I want You to make a way for me to take my family to Disney World. The kids are growing older each day, and the window of wonder is closing faster and faster. And I want to share this with them as a family."

At the time, my daughter was seven years old and my son

was six. I left that prayer (along with a couple bolder asks) in my living room and went about my normal life. The dishes were calling my name. Well, let's be honest. The dishes were always calling my name, and I ignored them just like the day before. However, I had to pick up the kids from school, make sure the milk was fresh, and cook dinner so that I could add to the ever-growing dish pile on the counter and in the sink. As I lay my head on my pillow that night, I knew and trusted that whatever God's answer—yes, no, or wait—I would continue to hope in Him. Besides, I have a long track record with hearing from God in one of those ways. And, ultimately, faith is a choice to trust even when the answer isn't favorable to you because you believe that the One you're asking is Favor Himself. Whether His answer is yes, no, or wait, I choose to esteem God as innately good.

Two weeks later, the video went viral, and I went from wrestling with feeling unseen to being seen by millions. Overnight, I was receiving call upon call and request upon request to be a guest on different media outlets. Some interviews gave me the opportunity to travel, occasionally with my entire family.

Just a few days after the viral video, I answered my phone yet again. And when the caller identified herself, I almost dropped my phone: It was the director of all Disney parks with a special request. Are you kidding me? Could I really be talking to this person over the phone right now? Oh, don't think for one second that my prayer wasn't in the forefront of my mind as I began to engage in this conversation.

Now, because Disney World had a section wholly devoted to the fans of *Star Wars*, they wanted me to come and film a small digital short advertising that area and offered for my family to come along. To say that I kept my junk together at that moment would be the biggest lie I've ever told. I found myself on the phone with a complete stranger, crying my eyes out in gratitude. Even now I can feel every emotion; my knees weakened and I hunkered down on the floor trying to collect words like "thank you" and "you have no idea what this means to me" while my voice stuttered through tears.

And do you know what this sweet soul did then? She cried with me. If you've never cried with a stranger over the phone, it is one of the most exhilarating and awkward moments I can promise you'll ever experience. She informed me that she wanted me to dream up the big things we didn't want to miss at Disney World while we were there and she would take care of the rest.

Within twenty-six days of that bold and frustrated prayer with the Maker of the Universe over a seemingly long-shot wish list, I now had a direct line with the director of the Magic Kingdom asking me for another wish list.

So, we now had to explain to our kids that there was indeed a real-life castle the mirror image of the one that played in the logo before all their favorite movies. But we didn't want to spoil the full surprise yet. So, we lied some more. Oh guys, don't hate me. We told our kids to find Disney World pictures and videos online and then create a park replica in our home for a fun family weekend. We told them to pack their suitcases for our pretend trip. We gathered intel on what rides they thought would be the most fun. My daughter even took several sheets of notebook paper and drew a sign for every individual attraction they wanted to pretend to ride and taped them throughout the house. Can you tell she is my daughter? It reminded me of all those paper skyscrapers I made when I was her age. Except this time, I knew for sure I was going to take her to the real place and blow her mind.

Can we pause here? Did you see that? Not only did God hear my prayer as a momma, but He showed up in my past and present to tell me He had seen my whole life. I hadn't fully seen His goodness and work in such a personal way until that moment. As I watched my daughter dream in paper, I felt the full heart of a momma with a surprise waiting around the corner that our little girl couldn't even imagine if she tried. Immediately, I heard a whisper inside that I believe was a thought from God to me revealing His nature as the "good Father" I had been doubting. It's as if I heard Him say, "Candace, baby girl, I saw your paper dreams as well. I have been waiting for this moment for so long to share this surprise with you. I love you so much. I didn't want to spoil the surprise for you either." I fully believe God was reminding me that there wasn't a day He wasn't near me—seeing me, hearing me.

The morning we left for Florida, we told the kids it would be fun to take those packed bags to the airport and watch planes take off. Then, once we got there, we told them the truth. We were really going to the Disney World we had been pretending and dreaming about. It would be an understatement to say there weren't a few hundred tears as we went through security checkpoints and watched their reactions as the reality of what we told them sank in.

When we landed in Florida, we were greeted by a Disney VIP tour guide in a plaid vest and dapper straw hat holding a sign imprinted with our family's last name. As we waited to retrieve our luggage from the carousel, the guide asked each of our children their favorite Disney character. My daughter responded with the obvious answer we have long known as a family: Belle. My little girl is a bit of a bookworm herself and has always loved that commonality with the beautiful Belle. Then our guide, Mr. Anthony, turned to our son and asked the same question.

Now, our son replied with an answer we weren't expecting. Duncan has always loved the villain. Always. For some strange reason, he likes Scar more than Simba, Darth Vader more than Luke Skywalker, and Captain America more than Iron Man. (I know. That last comparison was a bit of a jab for true Marvel fans. I do not apologize. Okay, maybe I will. Once you join Team Iron Man.) However, Duncan's answer was a Disney character that we'd rarely ever heard him talk about.

Out of his charming little mouth came the answer: Buzz Lightyear. Hmmm. That was unexpected. Chris and I raised our eyebrows at each other. Kids are full of surprises, I guess.

But then it was time to load our luggage in our tour

guide's company car. We checked into one of the fanciest rooms they had to offer. It had hidden Mickey Mouse silhouettes within the wallpaper, a balcony of our own that we would eventually watch fireworks from, and a welcome basket with Disney World memorabilia for the whole family. Given passes to any of the four parks in the world of Disney for the next four days, we dropped our bags and met Mr. Anthony back in the lobby. He accompanied us everywhere as our own personal golden ticket. We parked in the back lot where cast members would enter and didn't have to wait in line for any ride that we wanted to ride.

As we came through a back entrance, wouldn't you know it? The very first character in costume we spotted was good old Buzz Lightyear. Duncan instantly flipped out. "Mom! Dad! Look! It's Buzz Lightyear!"

Buzz himself was there to escort us personally into the Buzz Lightyear ride as the first step of our family's Disney adventure. Space cruisers, laser canons, and a galactic space battle—we loved every second of it! And we loved everything else the park had to offer.

We found ourselves in the front row for the Main Street parade where I captured on camera the first of many moments when I saw the light inside my children's eyes, including a picture of my daughter that served as wallpaper on my cell phone for months after. She was watching the float that ushered in Beauty and the Beast, of course. We ate to our hearts' content, trained to become Jedi masters, felt our stomachs drop to our toes on a ride called the Tower of Terror as we plunged several stories to the ground (twice!), and went on a nighttime safari to visit the real-life Lion King. We went from ride to ride, with our gracious tour guide parting the seas of people and expertly leading every step of the way. Our kids had gone from ignorance of such a place to the assumption that it was a glamorous and easygoing experience with the royal treatment. (I'm pretty sure we'll have to burst that expectation bubble the next time we go.)

As Mr. Anthony led us through the parks and had meals with us, I noticed other employees would pull him aside and engage in serious conversations. I wasn't nosy enough to listen in, but I could tell something was up through their body language. His friends and coworkers would gently grasp his shoulder or tilt their heads with sympathetic looks on their faces.

Nevertheless, he was all smiles as he escorted our family through the most joy-filled four days I can remember.

It's crazy to think how you can grow to love another person like a family member in just a few short days, but we did. We loved our new friend in the plaid vest. Mr. Anthony was more than just heads above the crowd by his tall stature; he was calm and reserved and had a heart that felt like a warm hug. He'd engage our kids in conversations that would draw out their smiles and giggles. He told me a friend had sent him the Chewbacca Mom video, and we told him about the wild tales that had happened since.

However, something in me knew there was more hidden behind Mr. Anthony's joy offerings to our family, something behind his eyes that I knew as intimately as I had known in my quest to make others laugh in college . . . a hidden sorrow. I didn't know the cause of the pain he was suppressing, but I knew it was present. And I knew whatever was there was his to share or keep.

As our magical journey through the Disney parks continued, the movie *Inside Out* (yes, the same one we discussed earlier in the book) kept coming to mind as I gauged Mr. Anthony's reactions to coworkers and friends.

I am about to reveal some movie spoilers, so get ready. (You may want to put a bookmark in these pages, pop a bucket of popcorn, and rent the film before going any further.) There's something special about the characters Joy and Sadness when they get together. They seem like total opposites, and yet they complement each other well. The movie brilliantly reflects the need to have both emotions present to be emotionally healthy. The secret to an abundant life is knowing how to embrace each. Otherwise, the lack of hope gives birth to despair. And when desperation grows, it leads to despairing acts.

In the movie, we see this play out as a young child rationalizes that she can overcome all her sorrow and fear by abandoning her loved ones, escaping her realities, and running away from the safety and protection of her home. And so, she goes. But don't worry. Once she embraces both Joy and Sadness, the little girl comes to her senses and rushes home before making it too far from her family.

After we first saw the film, I loved it so much that my

husband bought me a stuffed doll version of the character Sadness. If you press her palm, she says a variety of phrases from the film. One of my favorites: "Find the fun? I don't think I know how to do that."

Isn't that like most of us? We are in a struggle to find the fun in a world of sadness. Yet, there's one thing I want you to know about my friend Joy. She doesn't let you cry alone, and she doesn't let you cry for long.

Now, I am not one who looks for God under every rock or in every nook and cranny. Sometimes I see the hand of God at work very clearly. Other times, I feel as though I am searching for Him through a thick fog that would rival those in a Stephen King novel turned into an eighties movie.

However, on our final day at Disney, I believe God showed up in a very unexpected way. At last, we had arrived at the best animatronic ride in the history of all rides, with the catchiest tune you've ever heard. Yes, that's the sound of sarcasm in my voice. You guessed it: It's a Small World. It's not at *all* annoying. I mean, you only get in a boat to float through a staged animatronic world with the same tune playing over and over again. Sometimes I have nightmares with those animatronics in them. They don't ever come close to me. They just do what they do best: move and tilt their plastic, robotic heads back and forth, and hum their God-forsaken tune hours on end. Did I mention it doesn't stop? The maddening music has no end. Zip, zilch, nada. Nevertheless, it's an iconic Disney World ride that cannot be missed, and I knew good ole Grandma would inevitably ask the kids if they rode it when we got back to Texas. Lord forbid we didn't give them the opportunity to be as jacked up by the experience as we were! Plus, I had the mild curiosity to see if the ride had changed any from my childhood memories of it.

And wouldn't you know it? This was the ride where I would hear from God. I know, I know. I've asked Him over and over again why He had to use *that* ride and, what I had wrongly assumed to be, that God-forsaken song. As I hummed along (seriously—you hate it, and then you can't help it), I intentionally thought about the lyrics: It's a world of tears and fears but also a world of hope and laughter.

As we sat in that ridiculous toy boat and the lyrics swirled in my head, I began to tear up. I felt I was hearing God acknowledge that He opened the door for my life to be a catalyst to help others "find the fun" when they "didn't know how to do that." God had broken through my fears and tears with this robust laugh within me as I enjoyed a simple toy mask quite literally for the entire world to hear and share. And, in His eyes, from a higher perspective, it was a small world after all. So small, in fact, that overnight, the entire world could be reached with joy breaking through their computers and cell phone screens.

Surrounded by dancing flowers and terrifying, singing child robots, I felt this overwhelming sense that I was loved and useful for a new purpose. I knew without a doubt that when I had asked God to honor my wants as well as my needs just weeks earlier, He heard me. I was known and seen more than I could probably ever imagine. All things that I had long dreamed and hoped for were leading me to new, destined moments to share joy with a world of sadness. And I could sense this was much bigger than any dream I could dream for myself. I sensed it as I walked through crowds of people wanting to stop and share their stories of how my video changed their life or lifted their spirits. I even sensed it in Mr. Anthony's smiles. With each passing day, more light was peering through the hidden darkness in his eyes.

Finally, it was time to leave. We were genuinely sad to say goodbye to Mr. Anthony in our hotel lobby. So was he. However, there was more sadness to uncover than just the sorrow from parting ways with new pals. I could tell he had something to inform us that was important to him; that he wanted to reveal what was plaguing his thoughts and striving to steal his joy. I also sensed whatever he was about to share was difficult to say aloud.

With tears streaming gently down his face, he explained that this was the first time he had been back to work since his brother died unexpectedly a few weeks earlier and that he was still lost in grief. He had watched my viral video because he had lost the ability to laugh or even smile since his brother's death. He confessed that he had tried defiantly not to laugh—but that he wasn't successful.

I glanced down to release a tear of my own and noticed he was holding a plastic bag. Mr. Anthony shared with us that his late brother was an avid collector of his personal favorite Disney character. And wouldn't you guess it? His brother's favorite character was none other than Buzz Lightyear.

Earlier that day, during our family's nap time, our tour guide went to his late brother's home, grabbed a collectible, and brought it for Duncan. He pulled out the vintage Buzz action figure with parachute, still neatly in its original box. You would have thought there was nothing that would rival the experiences we had just had as a family at Disney World, but Duncan was just as joyful to receive this gift as he was to ride the Tower of Terror earlier that day. Duncan didn't understand fully how special, and I assume difficult, that gift was to give. Yet his reaction could convince you otherwise. He lit up and hugged Mr. Anthony and didn't take his eyes or hands off his new favorite toy in the history of all toys ever given to him: a vintage parachute Buzz Lightyear.

I believe God even used my son to bring some comfort and joy in the most unexpected way to Mr. Anthony that day, just as he had given so much joy to us. As Duncan's parents who had rarely heard of a love for Buzz Lightyear, we dismissed it as a random confession. However, to our hurting and grieving friend, it was a meaningful connection to someone he loved.

I was humbled, looking back, that our tour guide led us through the weekend while expressing a whole slew of wide-ranging emotions. He laughed with us as we watched our children fearlessly tackle rides that made me terrified. He smiled with us when Cadence refused to be the last to let go in every embrace of a newfound costumed Disney character. And, quietly and to the side, he took emotional punches as he received condolences from friends on his first day back to work. He'd been leading us through a tour of joy and grief. Which is a lot like life, isn't it?

Grief is a part of the fullness of life that we cannot ignore or overstep. Life can bring loss and pain, and we need lament to get honest about these experiences and how they shape us. The moments we honestly accept our loss and heartache are just the right moment for Joy to step in with hope and comfort. What memory must have flooded Mr. Anthony's mind as he met Duncan by the baggage claim and his first words were a connection and reminder of the brother he had just lost? What sorrow must he have felt as we stumbled upon the Buzz Lightyear ride and Buzz in costume giving hugs outside its entry gate as our first attraction? Then, what joy it was to see a small child light up with wonder and a mother and father swoon with gratitude as they connected to that same character as well! God writes the moments of joy with memories of sadness all too beautifully, if only we will make a little space to receive all the emotions we were created to own.

No, my dear friends. Joy won't let you cry alone, and she doesn't let you cry for long. Sincerely, there is comfort that waits within and on the other side of your tears. If no one has told you already, I hope you'll hear it from me: You got this. This is not the end. You're going to be okay. One day soon, you will have the know-how and will find the fun again. In the meantime, cry as many tears as it takes. Take as much time as you need. Just know that Joy hasn't left your side. Joy is here for you with comfort even in your sorrow, and with hope to help you up again when you're ready.

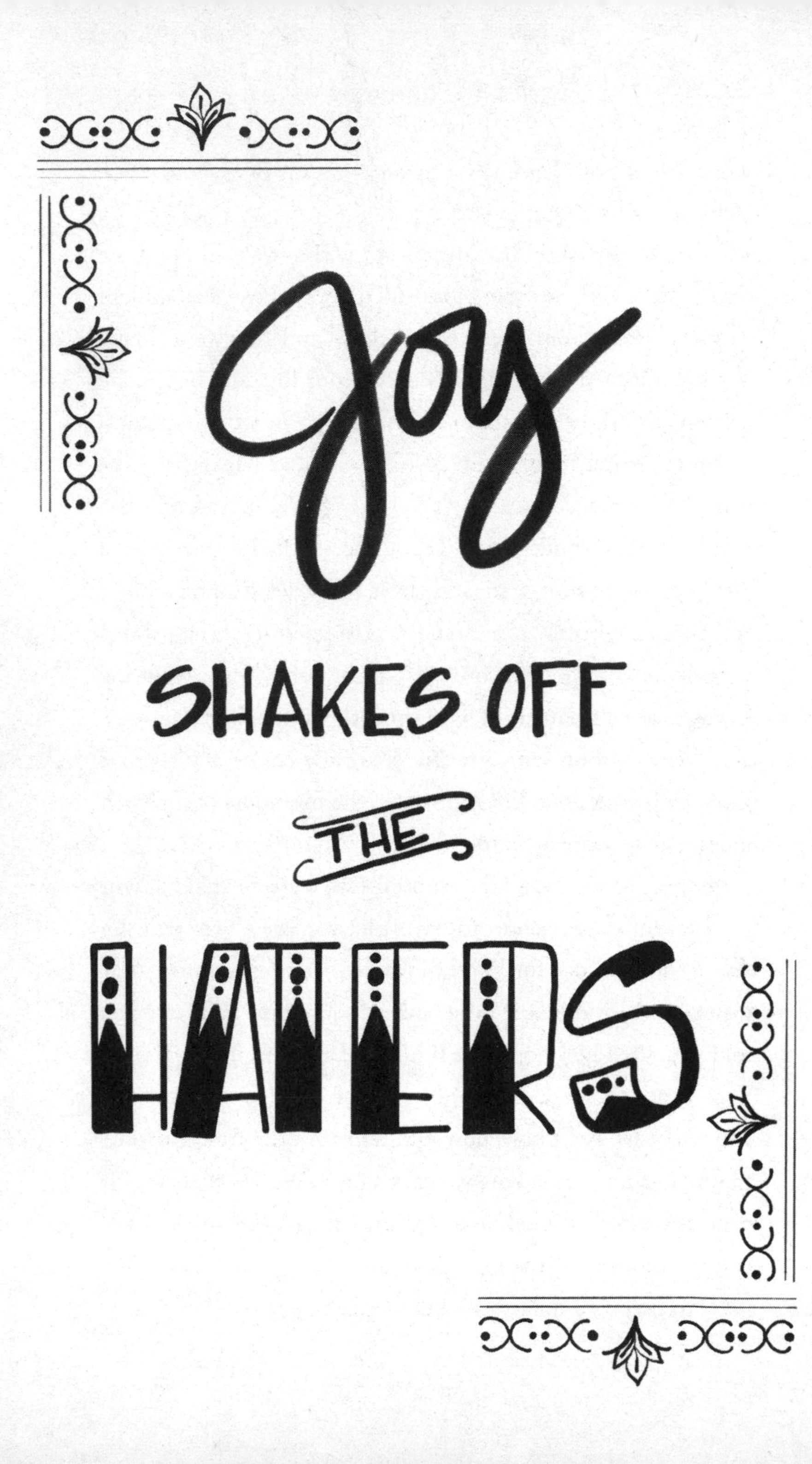
Joy
SHAKES OFF
THE
HATERS

Chapter 10

LATER, HATER

As opportunities to share my joy with the world grew greater and greater, the world around me, very close to me, in fact, grew more in need of comfort than I have seen in ages. Yes, even in those months following the video, there were very real fears and tragedies happening near and far. As an American, we had just celebrated our independence on the Fourth of July. Nearly seven weeks after the world had responded to the Chewbacca Mom video with laughter and acceptance, our nation was torn by racial tension, shocked and saddened by the killings of Alton Sterling and Philando Castile. What was intended as a peaceful protest in my hometown, Dallas, Texas, turned into an evening of panic and open shooting in our streets. I live less than twenty-five miles from where officers and civilians lost their lives. The nation we had just celebrated was turning on itself in ugly violence.

I woke up two days after the shootings in my hometown feeling intense sorrow and heaviness. The grief I felt wasn't political in nature, because politics belong to a nation. (I am not one to openly discourse about my political opinions. I haven't felt the need or pressure to share those discussions outside of my home.) I was thinking more of the entire world we share, this world with its very real tears and fears. I was looking past our borders to the basic needs we all have for love, acceptance, and freedom. And I thought as I pondered what kind of world we are leaving for our children, *Has hate's voice become stronger than love's?*

Any time lives are lost, we are left to wonder and grieve all we could have done to prevent it. So that mothers wouldn't have to lose their sons or daughters. So that wives wouldn't have to lose their husbands. So that we wouldn't be left with so much loss and emptiness. I felt this unseen assault ambushing humanity. I wanted to do something . . . I just didn't know what. The only thought that swirled in my mind was that I had a voice. And sometimes, that's all you have.

As I got dressed that morning, I began humming to myself an old Michael Jackson song, "Heal the World." A bit later, sitting at my piano while my family finished their morning routine, I looked at the time on my phone and felt an urge to go live with the words that were swirling from my mind to my heart. I didn't care about if I sounded perfect or beautiful. I wanted to sing those lyrics over families facing loss, a nation divided, homes hurting, and hearts broken. I wanted to remind whoever would watch and listen that we have a choice every day to make the world a better place. It was a call to action for those who felt powerless to their situation, especially to the senseless violence that had been displayed on our home television screens and social media feeds. It's an anthem to hope. And so I sang.

I ended the live broadcast, helped my kids tie their shoes, and went about my day running errands and showing our children that life was made for savoring and making memories. Within hours, I started seeing notifications that this video was going viral as well. Most people responded positively and encouraged me with grateful, heartfelt sentiments. However, unlike the love I felt from the Chewbacca Mom video, on a small scale I now began to know the sound of internetweb trolls and haters.

I remember seeing an unidentified phone number cross my screen. It's always like a mental game of Russian roulette when that happens. To answer the unknown caller or let it go to voicemail? That is the question. Well, that day I was feeling pretty adventurous, so I answered what turned out to be a press inquiry from the *New York Times* asking how I felt about the opposition to my post. If there was ever a moment I wished I hadn't been feeling adventurous, it was right then. My aim is spreading joy, so I didn't want even to dwell on or give a stage to the negativity. (Here's a tool and a trick: IGNORE. Seriously. There's so much freedom when you allow it to roll right off your back.)

Nevertheless, I had a somewhat persistent journalist on the line wanting my opinion. I'm not a jerk, so I offered this quote that I still believe to be true: "When a fire blazes in our personal lives, we all hold a bucket in our hands. It's what is in that bucket that makes all the difference. You can choose to have either water (to quench the fire) or gasoline (to fuel and stoke the flames). As far as it can be with me, I will always have water in my bucket."

It wasn't a big deal to me that I had taken to my social media outlets to offer hope and healing through song; however, it did seem to be a big deal to others. Some commented, "Why does Chewbacca Mom need to weigh in on something as serious as this?" Other commenters were under the illusion that I had only sung to try to keep alive any fifteen minutes of fame that I had earned. Only those who know me beyond the online snippets understand how hurtful that accusation was.

As I mentioned earlier in the book, I have been known as a singer and songwriter to my core group of friends for all my life. Taking to the lens of my phone and posting a video singing wasn't a new thing. As a matter of fact, I have often felt most comfortable in my own skin as a singer, songwriter, and worship leader. I have spent years training vocally, learning how to communicate authentically and with one's whole heart in song.

Not to mention, this "fame" thing isn't even real. At the end of the day, I do laundry and dishes and clean toilets like every other mom in the history of moms. I haven't felt the heavy pressure of needing to maintain repute or spotlight because I know the door that opened to me was nothing I ever could chart, plan, or manipulate. Let's just revisit this thought about that viral video, shall we? It's a four-minute selfie with three minutes of laughing. I think that says all that's necessary about the intelligence and planning required to make a video go viral. Y'all. I couldn't have fabricated that moment in time if I hired a room full of Einsteins to calculate every aspect of what I should or shouldn't have done. Nevertheless, as Taylor Swift sings, "Haters gonna hate." (And if you're reading this, T-Swift, I heart you!)

We all have known a hater in life. They love social media. I've since learned to make the block button my favorite button on the internetwebs.

To be clear, I'm not speaking of critics. I appreciate dialogue, even with those who downright disagree with me . . . *if* we can carry on a conversation with mutual respect. We can learn a lot from one another when we engage those with opposite opinions, as long as love is the foundation. And it can be a good thing to have someone challenge our beliefs, providing us with the opportunity to think more deeply about them ourselves.

But there's a difference between critics and bullies. I can tell the difference easily, and I bet you can, too. Bullies are the ones who incite hateful sentiments for the sake of being hateful or to stir up drama. It's the cyber-bullies of the world who long for a stage and voice to speak whatever ugly is already in their hearts and minds. Unlike critics, these haters aren't interested in your side of the conversation at all. Rather, they're raising their voices to shut yours down.

It's ironic to me that the day I shared my "Heal the World" tribute, I met these folks in full force. And they definitely did not want to hear my voice.

If I am honest, I hope a few are reading this now. If

there's ever a group of people that my heart yearns to see experience authentic joy, it's them. I do not say that with an ounce of sarcasm or as a jab to anyone that has played that role online toward me. I do believe it is possible for the most hurt and hurtful individuals to experience a life of joy as well. As a matter of fact, I believe they are incredible candidates for being joy ambassadors. Usually, those with the strongest opinions coupled with the loudest voices are the ones who will be the best joy converts. There's something wonderful about seeing those who have turned from hate to love. I adore redemption. I admire those brave enough to change hearts of stone into hearts that are tender and vulnerable. And there's nothing better than a good turn-around story.

But, alas, until that repentant moment that people can only choose for themselves, hate can have a very real effect on our personal joy pursuit. The most common distraction to living a joy-filled life is to feel a need to play the defense instead of the offense. But true Joy doesn't need to defend herself to anyone, and we don't need to defend the motives of our heart to haters. It's never worth wasting our time or energy there, not when Joy is calling us to so much more.

Joy is an offensive player—not offensive in the sense that she stimulates and stirs up unfair judgment or demands, but offensive in the way that she runs the ball down the field to make a goal. When we allow our mind to dwell on negativity and hateful words, we are switching sides. We find ourselves in a battle of words and wits while countering attacks instead of preserving the goal of actually living full of joy. This, my sweet friends, is why I love the block button. I have to remain on the offense in my pursuit of joy daily. If I don't, I will easily be distracted by petty arguments and divisions, and all the while miss my aim.

If you're anything like me, you wish there was such a thing as a block button in real life, too. Because unfortunately, hateful words aren't limited to online. Like you, I have known the sting of hearing them face-to-face. Sometimes, these words are spoken from a place of ignorance or without thought. Sometimes, they are more a confession about the other person's character than your own.

For example, a church mentor from my past once "lovingly" corrected me for appearing in a video with the very talented, comedic Sean Hayes, who is gay. The individual went on and on about how I didn't need to associate myself with a person of this "type" if I truly wanted to represent Jesus. Ick! I was appalled! Are you kidding me? I'm quite sure I'm not the first to point this out, but Jesus was often critical of people who were so legalistic that they favored religion over the needs of the people around them. Jesus also spent most of his time loving the very people the religious leaders of the day wouldn't go near with a ten-foot pole.

Y'all. Hate is easy to spot yet hard to wash off. However, there comes a moment when you have to shake off hate and ignorance even if it's the only thing you've ever known or been taught.

Let's not forget that just a short while ago, I was living a life that was far from public, in the thick of anonymity.

In those years, I didn't give a front-porch seat to hatred and bullying. Why in the world should I feel the pressure to do so now? But don't think it wasn't a struggle for everything in me that loves to people-please. And don't misinterpret my confidence as my ability to ignore every detestable word with absolute grace and dignity. I only write with such passion and choose this to be the last thought I leave with you in your pursuit of joy because negativity can easily deter you from the course.

There is a subtle difference in accepting useful criticism and firing back full force as you rebuke critical attacks. Though I usually don't offer specific how-tos for achieving joy, in this case I want to share with you a skill I'm learning to use daily both online and offline in my fight with negative criticism. Because let's be honest: It's more a battle of the mind to remain positive and not succumb to negative thinking than it is a battle against the abstract thought of hatred. Mind doing a little exercise with me? I didn't think you would; you're the best.

Draw a small circle. Go ahead. Find an empty spot in this book or use a separate sheet of paper and then come back to this paragraph. It'll be worth it, I promise. Next, inside the circle list the closest and most loving relationships you have. This should not be a vast list, only the people who know you inside and out. (If you don't have room, write their names next to the circle and draw an arrow.) These are the people who have shown and earned trust to speak into your life with love. These people, your core people, are those to whom you would listen if they said something was off-kilter in your life. They are a good gauge that you may have offended, been in the wrong, or have acted irrationally.

Do you have your list in the circle? Cool.

Now, draw another circle outside the smaller circle. List in this circle the names of casual acquaintances. You see them from week to week and interact with them fairly often: the fellow regular at the coffee shop, the friend at the playground where you both take your kiddos, etc. Such individuals haven't earned the right to speak criticism into your life because they typically don't know you outside the one common routine you share. When anyone in this circle speaks hate, you don't completely dismiss it, but you keep it in check. Meaning, it could be okay to ask someone in your core if that criticism is accurate of you or not.

Are you with me, actually drawing circles and listing names? Or are you doing what I do with workout and exercise DVDs? Meaning, I usually grab a slice of pizza and drink soda while I admire how impressive the exercising looks. "Wowzers. She can lift her legs high, huh?" Yeah. Try to resist the urge merely to "observe." I need your full participation!

One last art assignment. Draw a large circle that encompasses anyone outside of your core circle and your casual circle. In this circle is everyone you do not know. Go ahead and draw a bunch of question marks to represent the voices that speak but should have no influence over your mind or heart. Rarely do I even entertain criticism from those in the last circle unless it resonates with my gut that it may be something I have long overlooked. If that happens, I bring the criticism to my core people and have them test it out for me, because they know and love me the best.

It's hard to discern criticism, y'all. We cannot immediately dismiss people. I wholeheartedly believe everyone has the right to think and believe whatever they choose.

But here's the bright side. A heart full of joy doesn't fear correction; it welcomes it, because correction offers us the opportunity to grow. We don't have to fear criticism because it's up to no one but us to decide if that remark is groundless or an opportunity for personal growth. I believe we can choose to accept words of critique as fuel to inspire us to change. I also believe we can dismiss and ignore the words altogether if they are empty, or vain, or unsolicited. Currently, I'm finding the circle chart that I keep in my head helps every single time as I discern which words to listen to and which to tune out and shake off.

Another lesson I am learning every single day and will continue to learn until I go to the grave is this: *Have a heart that isn't easily offended.* I cannot tell you the joy that comes rushing in when you figure this out! Sometimes the only thing stealing your joy is your adverse reaction to constructive criticism. OUCH! I know that may have been harsh to hear, especially if this idea is a foreign concept to you. But seriously. If no one has told you this ever or in a while, can I remind you? You have within you the power to decide how you'll react to criticism. And I'm not just siding with the old adage,

"Sticks and stones may break my bones, but words will never hurt me." Whoever said that wasn't thinking with their whole noggin. Words *do* hurt. They have the power to provoke life or death. Still, how much more amazing is it that we have even more power to take captive words that go against what we know to be true! I love how I have the ultimate say-so in how hurtful and spiteful words will affect my mind and direct my actions. Taylor Swift was really onto something when she sang, "Shake It Off." You may need to use your real-life block button to keep people from bullying you. I let people give me loving criticism all the time. But I don't give anonymous bullies a platform to abuse me as they see fit.

Ultimately, I was at a crossroads with what to do with the hateful criticism I received after posting my "Heal the World" video. I decided to fight back with positivity and do something more than just enter a verbal argument in a comment thread on Facebook. I wanted the video to count for all the reasons I cared to create it in the first place. I also chose not to incite argument or backlash in an interview with the media. Can you imagine the snowball of even more criticism that could have come from that? Imagine the headlines: "Chewbacca Mom Gets Feelings Hurt Over Online Criticism" or "Not Such a Happy Chewbacca Any Longer: A Glimpse into Chewbacca Mom's Media Outrage." Sheesh. Glad I avoided that. I also wanted to put action to the words I had sung courageously. I wanted to make the world a better place in a very tangible way.

I booked some music studio time and hired a team to

help me record the arrangement I sang online. I knew in my heart that I wanted to find an organization that was doing its part in making the world "a better place." I have known about the humanitarian organization Convoy of Hope for several years through my local church and other venues. Committed to helping feed millions of people in need in the United States and around the world, in the past twenty years Convoy of Hope has been active in forty-eight states, providing disaster response, conducting community outreach events, and directing nutritional programs and sustainability projects. They also have continuing programs in Haiti, El Salvador, the Philippines, Guatemala, Honduras, Tanzania, Nicaragua, Kenya, South Africa, and Ethiopia.

So, I decided to put my single of "Heal the World" on iTunes and donate all profits from sales to Convoy of Hope. Within the first day of release, the song charted number twenty-seven on the pop charts on iTunes. Can we just pause right there? Never did I ever imagine I would have a top-forty song on the pop charts! Mercy! (Never did I imagine when I got my first guitar years ago, a toy mask would be the culprit in seeing part of that dream come alive!) And that isn't just a humble brag. If I had chosen to cave to the criticism I heard online, children, women, and families that may have gone without needs met by the dollars donated to do the wonderful work Convoy of Hope is daily doing. Can I even tell you how much joy that gives me! Y'all. Holy moly! Sure, it's cool having a song chart on iTunes, but the real joy comes when you see human life rescued and restored! It is possible to overcome the voices of hate and replace them with joy. To this day and through the life of that song as it remains on iTunes, all profits will go to empowering women, feeding children, and offering hope and refuge to families facing natural disasters.

I don't dare presume I know the voices of hatred and discouragement that have bullied you online or offline. You may be in the middle of the fight for your life in trying to find a single thing positive under the weight and heaviness of all the hate you face daily. You may even be in a home, marriage, or job where you consistently fight to remain joyful and hold onto hope. I pray you will find the courage and gumption to block the voices of hate. I implore you to make the list of all the relationships that should give you pause when you may need to listen to healthy criticism.

Know this: Joy is on this journey with you. She hears you and sees you fighting for her to have a place in your life. Go ahead: Let Joy in and say, "Later, hater" to anything or anyone else trying to take her place.

Be offensive in your pursuits for joy.

Keep your circles of valued voices in the forefront of your mind when you do need to be defensive.

Hit that block button often, both online and in real life.

Cultivate a heart that doesn't get offended easily.

And, like I said in the "Heal the World" live video:

"MAKE A BETTER WORLD, Y'ALL. FILL IT WITH JOY, NOT HATE. C'MON."

Joy
Never
RUNS
OUT.

YOU'RE FULL OF IT

Joy is not only a journey to find and keep; it is a resource that you can deplete and replenish.

Throughout my life, I have seen Joy show herself in moments when least expected. I remember finding her hiding behind every tree stump and hidden trail we called our backyard while homeless in the woods. I remember feeling her warmth as the sunset hit my face while skipping rocks in the creek beds and fishing for tadpoles. I remember Joy's call to play even in days when the only food we knew were fried bologna sandwiches and cans of Vienna sausages. She would speak to my imagination, "Clean your plate! You don't want to be late for the fashion show Smurfette is about to debut!" I remember the nearness of Joy's playful spirit when I watched my mom skip out of the gas station with an eighty-nine-cent bag of Dum-Dum suckers to share so that each of her children could have a special treat when we couldn't afford dollar fifty scoops of ice cream.

I watched Joy stay the course when I met ridicule and

rejection for the first time. I remember how she held my hand through doubts and discouragement when others couldn't buy into my dreams. I watched her dance with me to my favorite songs in the bedroom without walls and saw her face light up when I learned my first guitar chord. Joy was in the room where I discovered to both fail and lead well as a worship leader after getting my first guitar. Joy watched me press in and practice on the porch of our single-wide trailer while the rest of my family slept. Joy dreamed the daydream with me and rested in the hope that it would one day become a reality.

Joy was there as I found myself waist-deep in Comparison, even when I chose Comparison over her for a time. I knew Joy intimately on the night I tried to take my life, especially when she held my hand through a best friend who walked me around my college campus until my despair turned to gratitude. She laughed with me as I ripped my pants down the entire inseam on first dates. She helped me see the beauty in who I am and was there when I finally accepted that *I am enough* and don't need to live in comparison to anything or anyone else.

Joy was present in my darkest memories. She was fighting for me when I was sexually abused, mindful of how my heart had suffered the loss of innocence. Joy rushed in like a flood the day I evicted Shame. She gave me a reason to trust without reservation and receive pure love from a man I am forever grateful to call my best friend and husband. Joy waited patiently for me to invite her back into my inner circle as I fought against her for years. Joy remained faithful in my wandering.

I remember the night Joy found a voice to sing a lullaby to my daughter, comforted her, and put her to sleep because I couldn't rest from the fear of losing my marriage. She was there in the moments my mind regained clarity from postpartum depression. Joy reminded me that everyone is afforded a bad day now and then and to always offer the benefit of the doubt. She was in the resolve to save my marriage as I penned the word *divorce* and set it on fire, and she was with Chris and me as we set out to rebuild our life stronger together.

And, how could I forget loving Joy as she introduced me to my cherished children for the first time? She wrapped them in swirls of light, beauty, and utter sweetness so that I couldn't give enough kisses if I tried. Joy held to the hope all was well and never spoke doom and gloom over their lives. Joy showed herself in their gurgles, smiles, first steps, and echoed in the sound of the swoosh found each time I heard their hearts beat with life in my womb. Joy combated my fears and once again gently rested in the hope that it was better to "wait and see," not "run ahead and assume the worst" in the days of uncertainty. Instead of fearing the what-ifs, she taught me to laugh without fear at the days ahead, no matter what waited in each one.

Joy was with me as I bought toilet paper and milk, potty-trained two toddlers only fourteen months apart in age, and felt overlooked and anonymous to the dreams I had once dreamed. She inspired me to dance through the mundane. She invited me to find time for the simplest of pleasures as I experienced a routine life. Joy beckoned me to cherish the times alone and showed me her best side shines like the stars when I serve others. Joy was in the smile of my sweet, dear grandma, Annie Mae.

Joy helped me shut the *should* up! I often imagine her with a roll of duct tape and a sly grin on her face just wishing I would start the *should* again. She silenced the voices of those who had long controlled how I viewed my role on this earth. I watched as she ran through my thoughts with net and cage in hand capturing every idea that would threaten to take her place.

I witnessed Joy walk hand in hand with grief and sorrow. I watched her cry tears and sweep up brokenness into her dustpan. I watched her comfort through the connection of Buzz Lightyear in the confession of a six-year-old. Joy was there to offer herself to infinity and beyond. She was determined never to let us cry alone or cry for long.

And I heard Joy's voice high above the sounds of hate and criticism that bulldozed down her path without empathy or consequence. I watched her stay composed and confident as she changed the atmosphere clouded by hate and destruction. Joy surprised me when she lived unoffended. She showed me that kindness and compassion was always a better choice for those who have lost sight of who she is.

Many days, it took every effort I had to find where Joy was hiding.

Some days, Joy was nearer than my own breath.

Through it all, there is one common truth to be learned about joy: You can either be empty or full of it. And the choice is always ours.

Now, here's the best part of living a life full of it.

Your joy becomes contagious to those around you. You become a Joy ambassador.

I could tell you story after story of how people said they couldn't help but laugh when they saw my video. And I believe it was more than laughter that was contagious. It was the voice of Joy crying out to any and all who would hear her invitation. When you're full of it, there's only one thing you can do: overflow. My hope for you is that you won't just be filled to the brim with Joy as you embark on this journey far after you leave these pages. My hope is that you will overflow and infect everyone around you. It's not just for the happy-go-lucky Disney fans or "Wookiee Moms." Joy isn't a frivolous luxury. Joy is able to push through the densest obstacles growing on the life path you're walking. Joy can replace a cup of tears with oceans of laughter. Joy can fill up the most cavernous soul in an instant. And don't worry. Joy is never in short supply. When you're running low or empty, pause and look for her breadcrumbs leading you through hidden forests and play places. I urge you, sweet friend, live life to the fullest you possibly can with Joy by your side.

Listen, I know. Life will put you to the test. It can be difficult and unexpected, heartbreaking and hope-challenging. But Joy is a fighter. And so are you.

So, go ahead—be full of it. In the face of all and any odds, let your joy be defiant. Live free and full in EVERY moment, and laugh it up!

A NOTE FROM CANDACE'S PASTOR

It started out to be just another Wednesday night. Candace was headed to church. But on her way, she felt prompted to stop at Popeyes chicken.

Candace went into Popeyes and ordered a small side of mashed potatoes and sat down. There was only one other lady in the whole place. As Candace ate, she said a silent prayer, "Lord, why am I here?" And the Lord said, "You're here for her."

So Candace started up a conversation with the lady. Come to find out, she was a mom to two grown kids who were in college. She said to Candace, "I'm working hard to help my kids achieve their dreams, even though I never got to go to college."

The woman got up to go to the restroom. And while she was gone, Candace felt prompted to take the twenty dollars out of her pocket and give it to the lady when she came back.

She felt like God wanted her to sow a seed into her dream to go to college.

Candace prayed, "God, I'd love to do that, but the twenty dollars in my pocket is the only grocery money I have for the week. How about I give her ten dollars and I keep ten dollars?"

God said, "Give her the whole twenty dollars."

When the lady returned, Candace gave her the twenty dollars and told her she wanted to sow into her dream. The lady started to cry, overwhelmed with the kind gesture.

Candace went back to her car and right before she started it, she sat quietly for a moment. And in that moment, God spoke to her one more time. "Candace, you didn't just sow into that lady's dream . . . you sowed into your own . . . Wait till you see what I'm about to do with YOU."

You know how I know this about Candace Payne? Because I'm her pastor. And five minutes after all this happened, she called me and told me the whole story.

Guess what happened the next day?

Candace bought a Chewbacca mask at Kohl's and made a Facebook Live video . . . and Chewbacca Mom was born.

This book is not a product of a video that went viral on a Thursday; it is a product of a twenty-dollar act of obedience that took place in a chicken joint on a Wednesday night.

Candace Payne is not just a fun, talented, entertaining woman. She is one of the deepest wells of true joy I've ever known. And her joy is contagious. I'm sure you have laughed out loud as you read this book. (I did.) But more importantly,

I trust you have learned how to live a life of authentic joy that can't be shaken or stolen.

Scott Wilson
Senior Pastor, The Oaks Church,
Red Oak, Texas

ACKNOWLEDGMENTS

Team Z—David Morris, Tom Dean, Alicia Kasen, Robin Barnett, Curt Diepenhorst, and Greg Clouse: Seriously, Zondervan, I love you. You came to the table believing in me and seeing behind the mask long before many others. I'm so grateful for your partnership in making this a reality.

And to my brilliant editor, Stephanie Smith: You get me. That alone is a hard task!

Jana Burson and Chris Ferebee: I'm forever grateful for your role and know this is just the beginning of where this road is going. Hold on. More is coming.

To my two blessed helpers, Paige Collins and Shanon Stow: I can never describe the love I have for you and how you both have challenged me to own every page and word with bold, confident, and defiant joy. You are more than coworkers. You're sisters and best friends. The love is real.

Jonathan Merritt: I am grateful for our Chuy's dinner breaks and the direction you have given. I can never fully describe how vital our days together were. To say I'm grateful for you is an understatement.

For my Scott and Jenni: You both have walked me through intense seasons of doubt, serious hurts, and cynicism with such grace and true friendship. Thanks for being a catalyst to seeing my joy restored and my faith strengthened.

Without my family, what book on joy could I write if it weren't for you? Mom and Dad, thank you for modeling joy every day. For my brothers and sister, we've lived through a lot and survived even more. Our stories and memories are always my favorites. There's not a single day I would ever trade that has been with you. I love you. I'm grateful for you.

And to my Rock and Anchor, I owe every page and every hour spent pouring into this project to you. Chris Payne, you are a man among men. You truly get what it means to be a husband and father. You champion every dream of mine as though you've seen it in your sleep as well. Thanks for the long hours afforded me to write this and spend our money on lattes, tacos, and pan-seared dumplings to make this a reality. You're my favorite.

And to my sweet Cadeebug and Duncan-Punkin. Thank you for showing me how to hear the call of Joy every day that I wake up and get to hear you call me "Momma." You invite me into places I long forgot and remind me to laugh it up daily. I love you!